Theophrastus' *Characters*

This book presents an introduction to the *Characters*, a collection of thirty amusing descriptions of character types who lived in Athens in the fourth century BCE. The author of the work, Theophrastus, was Aristotle's colleague, his immediate successor and head of his philosophical school for thirty-five years. Pertsinidis' lively, original and scholarly monograph introduces Theophrastus as a Greek philosopher. It also outlines the remarkable influence of the *Characters* as a literary work and provides a detailed discussion of the work's purpose and its connection with comedy, ethics and rhetoric.

Sonia Pertsinidis is a lecturer in Classics at The Australian National University.

Routledge Focus on Classical Studies

This new series, part of the Routledge Focus short-form programme, provides a venue for the most up-to-date research in the field of Classical Studies. The series covers a range of topics, from focussed studies on specific texts, figures, or themes, to works on wider issues.

Available titles:

Prophets, Prophecy, and Oracles in the Roman Empire: Jewish, Christian, and Greco-Roman Cultures
by Leslie Kelly

Theophrastus' *Characters*: A New Introduction
by Sonia Pertsinidis

For more information on the Routledge Focus programme, please visit our author information page: www.routledge.com/resources/authors/how-to-publish-with-us

Theophrastus' *Characters*
A New Introduction

Sonia Pertsinidis

Routledge
Taylor & Francis Group

LONDON AND NEW YORK

First published 2018
by Routledge

2 Park Square, Milton Park, Abingdon, Oxfordshire OX14 4RN
52 Vanderbilt Avenue, New York, NY 10017

Routledge is an imprint of the Taylor & Francis Group, an informa business

First issued in paperback 2020

British Library Cataloguing-in-Publication Data
A catalogue record for this book is available from the British Library

Library of Congress Cataloging-in-Publication Data
A catalog record has been requested for this book

ISBN: 978-1-138-24443-6 (hbk)
ISBN: 978-0-367-60705-0 (pbk)

Typeset in Times New Roman
by Apex CoVantage, LLC

Dedicated to Savva, Aristotle and Athena

Contents

Sources and abbreviations

Aristotle

APr. = *Prior Analytics*
EE = *Eudemian Ethics*
EN = *Nicomachean Ethics*
Phgn. = *Physiognomonica*
Po. = *Poetics*
Pol. = *Politics*
Rh. = *Rhetoric*

Plato

Phdr. = *Phaedrus*
Phlb. = *Philebus*
R. = *Republic*

Theophrastus

CP = *De causis plantarum* = *Explanations for plants*
DS = *De sens.* = *On sense perception*
HP = *Historia plantarum* = *Investigations into plants*
Ign. = *De igne* = *On fire*
Lap. = *De lapidibus* = *On stones*
Metaph. = *Metaphysics*
Vent. = *De ventis* = *On winds*

DL = Diogenes Laertius *Lives* = fr. 1 in FHSG.
FHSG = Fortenbaugh, W.W., P. M. Huby, R. W. Sharples and D. Gutas (eds). 1992. *Theophrastus of Eresus. Sources for his Life, Writings, Thought and Influence*, 2 vols (Leiden: E. J. Brill).
Fr. 100 = text 100 in FHSG.
Jebb-Sandys = Jebb, R.C.; 1870, revised by Sandys, J.E. 1909. Theophrastou charakteres. *The Characters of Theophrastus*. An English translation from

a revised text, with introduction and notes by R.C. Jebb; a new edition by J.E. Sandys 1979 (New York: Arno Press).

RUSCH II = Fortenbaugh, W. W. (ed.) 1985. *Theophrastus of Eresus. On his Life and Work* (New Brunswick and Oxford: Rutgers University Studies in the Classical Humanities).

RUSCH III = Fortenbaugh, W. W. (ed.) 1988. *Theophrastean Studies. On Natural Science, Physics and Metaphysics, Ethics, Religion and Rhetoric* (New Brunswick and Oxford: Rutgers University Studies in the Classical Humanities).

RUSCH VIII = Ophuijsen, J. van and M. van Raalte (eds). 1998. *Theophrastus. Reappraising the Sources* (New Brunswick and London: Rutgers University Studies in the Classical Humanities).

RUSCH IX = Fortenbaugh, W. W. and E. Schütrumpf (eds) 2000, *Demetrius of Phalerum. Text, Translation and Discussion* (New Brunswick and London: Transaction Publishers).

RUSCH XII = Fortenbaugh, W. W. and S. White (eds). 2004. *Lyco of Troas and Hieronymus of Rhodes. Text, translation and Discussion* (New Brunswick and London).

RUSCH XIII = Fortenbaugh, W. W. and S. White (eds). 2006. *Aristo of Ceos. Text, Translation and Discussion* (New Brunswick and London).

TS = Fortenbaugh, W. W. 2003. *Theophrastean Studies.* (Stuttgart: Franz Steiner Verlag).

Preface

The *Characters* is one of the most unique, enjoyable and influential texts to have survived from the ancient Greek world yet, paradoxically, it is one of the least well-known works of ancient Greek literature. Theophrastus, the author of the work, was Aristotle's colleague and immediate successor. He was also head of Aristotle's philosophical school for more than three decades and an important philosopher and scientist in his own right. In the *Characters*, Theophrastus describes thirty character types living in ancient Athens in the fourth century BCE. Each type embodies a negative trait such as flattery, arrogance or surliness. Theophrastus illustrates these traits via a series of masterfully presented examples of speech and conduct. The result is an entertaining and instructive picture of a group of Athenian citizens. For classicists, the *Characters* offers a valuable insight into Theophrastus' approach to ethics and comedy and a unique window into certain social values. For literary historians, the work illustrates early concepts of 'character' and 'comic types' that had an extraordinary and long-lasting influence on character writing and comedy. For general readers, the *Characters* provides fascinating information on social etiquette and interaction in ancient Greek society.

This book seeks to introduce the *Characters* to a wider audience and to present a new perspective on the purpose of the work. It is motivated by a belief that the *Characters* deserves to be more widely known. Apart from being highly entertaining, the *Characters* is also a deceptively simple work with a complex ethical subtext. This book seeks to familiarise readers with the author and his work, to place the *Characters* in context, to synthesise the latest scholarship on Theophrastus and his contributions, and to offer new arguments on how the *Characters* relates to ethics, comedy and rhetoric. Although I have written this book with classical scholars, teachers and university students in mind, it also caters to those teaching and studying in the fields of history, literature, philosophy and drama as well as non-specialists and general readers.

As an introduction to the *Characters*, readers may wish to consult this book before, alongside or after reading the primary text. There are many translations of the *Characters* available. Diggle's edition (Oxford 2004) represents the most recent text and translation and it includes an extensive and helpful commentary. The Loeb edition (Cambridge Mass., London: 1993, 2002) is widely available both in print and online and the translation is lively and accurate. The Penguin edition usefully contains a translation of Theophrastus' *Characters* along with plays and fragments of the comic playwright Menander (Penguin Books, London 1967). There is also Sir Richard Claverhouse Jebb's edition (London and Cambridge, 1870), a delightful example of nineteenth-century scholarship and translation.

This book relies on the recent edition by Diggle. In consideration of readers without knowledge of ancient Greek as well as non-specialists, Greek words are translated or transliterated in the text and quotations are translated or explained. References are to scholarly works in English where possible. Throughout this book, I use *Characters* to refer to the complete work and 'character portraits' to refer to the thirty studies that make up the work. All titles and text references correspond to Diggle's edition.

My interest in this topic began many years ago (in 2001) at a summer history course at Cambridge University entitled 'Power and Exploitation in Ancient Greece'. I am grateful to the lecturer, Paul Millett, for mentioning the *Characters* in one of his lectures and for inadvertently setting me upon this long and fascinating journey. For offering useful comments and suggestions in reviewing my proposal, I would like to thank Amy Davis-Poynter from Routledge, David Mirhady of Simon Fraser University, Tad Brennan of Cornell University and the other anonymous reviewers. I offer special thanks to Han Baltussen of the University of Adelaide, who read a complete draft and very kindly gave suggestions on each chapter. I also offer my sincere thanks to Dianne Dean and Savva Pertsinidis for providing feedback and advice. Any remaining errors are entirely my own.

I thank my colleagues at the Centre for Classical Studies at the Australian National University, particularly Elizabeth Minchin, for her exceptional mentoring and guidance, and the wonderful classicists who have inspired me since my early days as an undergraduate: Douglas Kelly (†), my mentor and friend, who will forever represent the spirit of Greek philosophy, Ann Moffatt, who inspired me with her love of Greek art and drama, and Robert Barnes, who introduced me to the power and majesty of ancient rhetoric. Thanks also to my dedicated and enthusiastic students, especially those who translated the *Characters* with me in Advanced Greek (Semester Two, 2017).

Without doubt, I owe the biggest debt of gratitude to my family: to my sister Sophia, and to my mother-in-law Kalliope, for their support and encouragement, to my wonderful husband, Savva, for his endless patience, love and encouragement, and to our beautiful children, Aristotle and Athena, two miniature characters who fill our lives with plentiful examples of inappropriate behaviour and wonderful humour.

Sonia Pertsinidis
December 2017
Australian National University

Introduction

Theophrastus, the author of the *Characters*, was Aristotle's colleague, immediate successor and head of the Athenian philosophical school known as the Peripatos from 322 to approximately 289 BCE.[1] Theophrastus was an extraordinary polymath whose scholarly interests included the subjects of botany, biology, ethics, psychology, religion, politics, rhetoric, poetics and music. Two of Theophrastus' works in particular, *Explanations for Plants* and *Investigations into Plants*, established his place in history as the father of botany. The influence of Theophrastus' work in the sphere of literature has been even greater, owing to his unique book known as the *Characters*. Essentially, the *Characters* is a collection of thirty brief literary vignettes of middle- to upper-class Athenian male citizens. Each character exemplifies an undesirable behavioural trait. The titles of the characters provide a useful overview of the work. They are as follows:

1 The Dissembler	16 The Superstitious Man
2 The Toady	17 The Ungrateful Grumbler
3 The Chatterbox	18 The Distrustful Man
4 The Country Bumpkin	19 The Offensive Man
5 The Obsequious Man	20 The Disagreeable Man
6 The Man Who Has Lost All Sense	21 The Man of Petty Ambition
7 The Talker	22 The Illiberal Man
8 The Rumour-Monger	23 The Boastful Man
9 The Shameless Man	24 The Arrogant Man
10 The Penny-Pincher	25 The Coward
11 The Repulsive Man	26 The Oligarchic Man
12 The Tactless Man	27 The Late Learner
13 The Overzealous Man	28 The Slanderer
14 The Obtuse Man	29 The Friend of Villains
15 The Self-Centred Man	30 The Shabby Profiteer

The *Characters* was probably written shortly after the death of Alexander the Great, around 319 BCE.[2] This was a time of political upheaval in Athens and a lengthy power struggle between Macedonian-controlled oligarchs and democratic leaders.[3] But the world of the *Characters* and the world of politics rarely intersect[4] and only one of Theophrastus' character types has obvious political leanings (the *Oligarchic Man*). The remaining characters busy themselves with the sorts of everyday activities that preoccupied Athenian citizens in the late fourth century: shopping in the bustling marketplace; talking in the streets; visiting public venues such as the theatre, courthouse and assembly; frequenting festivals and games; and attending the public baths and gymnasia. In the private domain, the characters are shown interacting with wives, lovers, slaves and hired workmen, as well as managing properties, hosting dinners and tending to pets.

Each character portrait consists of a catalogue of inappropriate conduct and speech. The *Chatterbox*, for example, rambles on incessantly without considering his listener at all (3.2–4). The *Penny-Pincher* counts the number of cups that his guests drink at dinner and refuses to give salt to his neighbour (10.3, 13). The *Ungrateful Grumbler* cannot accept any good news, however remarkable it may be, without finding something to complain about (17.2–9). The *Boastful Man* is constantly exaggerating his wealth and status in an effort to impress others (23.2–9). There are also examples of inappropriate dress, such as the *Country Bumpkin* who slops around wearing over-sized shoes (4.2), and examples of inappropriate gestures, such as the *Offensive Man* who wipes his nose while eating (19.5).

At the heart of this work lies a perplexing question: why would a philosopher of the fourth century write a book of *Characters*? Although Theophrastus' purpose in writing the *Characters* has been discussed at length, it has proven difficult to pin down. Previously, scholars have tried to classify the *Characters* as belonging to a single field of study such as ethics,[5] comedy,[6] rhetoric[7] or science,[8] prompting intense scholarly debate.[9] This approach appears to have been based on an assumption that there were rigid divisions between different fields of study in the Peripatetic school and that the *Characters* emerged from only one field of study. In fact, Theophrastus and the other Peripatetics were not 'specialists' in the modern sense of the word.[10] They had broad interests covering an astonishingly diverse range of subjects. The study of ethics, for example, overlapped with law, politics, religion, comedy, psychology and rhetoric.[11] A fresh perspective on the *Characters* is possible if we view Theophrastus as a multidisciplinary researcher.

The central argument of this book is that the *Characters* is the product of a convergence of two main subjects: ethics and comedy. Like Aristotle, Theophrastus recognised the importance of ethical behaviour as central to a happy and blessed life.[12] He also accepted Aristotle's famous doctrine of the 'golden mean', which advocated avoidance of behavioural extremes and the pursuit of ethical conduct relative to the circumstances.[13] But Theophrastus was also an eminently practical philosopher who recognised that an abstract and philosophical discussion of virtue and vice can lack realism and appeal. He therefore devised the *Characters*: a set of amusing, realistic and vivid illustrations of 'bad' behaviour that simultaneously imply a model of 'good' behaviour. In this way, the character descriptions are both amusing and instructive and, by using comedy as the vehicle for his ethical teaching, Theophrastus makes the subject of ethics engaging and meaningful for everyday life. One of the delightful and surprising aspects of Theophrastus'

work is that centuries later these observations about human behaviour still resonate with audiences and still give rise to humour.[14]

Theophrastus achieves a synthesis between ethics and comedy in the *Characters* by means of several distinct and observable methods (Chapters 3 and 4).
By compressing examples of inappropriate speech and conduct into individual
episodes, Theophrastus creates a deliberately exaggerated portrait of his various
character types. The comedic effect is further amplified through the use of rhetorical devices, quoted speech and comic punchlines. At the same time, Theophrastus'
comedy has an important and serious purpose, appropriately summarised in Theophrastus' succinct definition of comedy as a 'concealed rebuke for error'. The
'errors' of the character types are the inappropriate forms of speech and conduct
that they unconsciously engage in. By demonstrating how a lack of self-awareness manifests in absurd and embarrassing ways, Theophrastus encourages people
to become more aware of their own conduct and that of others.

In short, I maintain that Theophrastus uses comedy as an effective and engaging vehicle for his ethical teaching. By giving clear illustrations of poor conduct, inappropriate speech, behavioural follies, bad timing and misjudgements,
Theophrastus underscores the importance of appropriate and well-timed social
behaviour. Although the *Characters* only describes negative behavioural traits, it
nevertheless implies what the respectable Athenian citizen should look like and
how he should behave and speak. In fact, the whole success of the work depends
upon this shared understanding of respectable conduct and social etiquette, which
makes Theophrastus' work especially valuable for studies of social values and
ethics in late fourth-century Athens.

Aims of this book

Any reader approaching Theophrastus' *Characters* for the first time will no doubt
have a multitude of questions: who was Theophrastus? When and why did he
write the *Characters*? In what way is the work significant? Why does it only portray negative character traits? How has the work been influential? The overarching aim of this book is to provide clear and succinct answers to these questions in
a manner that is suitable for both a scholarly and general audience.

Until now, a clear yet detailed introduction to the *Characters* has been lacking.
For several centuries, scholarship on the *Characters* has been preoccupied with
resolving difficulties with the text arising from the 'notoriously corrupt' manuscript tradition.[15] Many editions and translations of the *Characters* have been produced but the introductory remarks are often (necessarily) brief.[16] Diggle's recent
edition represents the best introduction and in-depth commentary produced to
date.[17] There are also detailed studies written by preeminent classical scholars,
such as Fortenbaugh and Millett, but these scholars assume a level of familiarity with Theophrastus and the *Characters* and they do not write with a general
readership in mind.[18] Outside of classical scholarship, there are useful works by
literary historians such as Gordon, Boyce and Smeed, who have traced the literary

influence of the *Characters*.[19] This book aims to fill the gap by providing a clear and comprehensive response to key questions that any reader might have about the text, especially questions pertaining to the author, context, influence, content, purpose and style of the work.

A key premise of this book is that Theophrastus was a significant philosopher whose life, works and influence have been to a large extent overshadowed by those of his teacher and colleague, Aristotle. For this reason, Chapter 1 is devoted to answering the question, 'Who was Theophrastus?' and demonstrating Theophrastus' significance as member, and later director, of the philosophical school established by Aristotle. Chapter 1 discusses Theophrastus' life, his works, his methodology and his own background as a philosopher, scientist and non-Athenian. This discussion forms an important backdrop to our study of Theophrastus' *Characters*.

Chapter 2 sets out to demonstrate the significant and enduring impact of Theophrastus' *Characters* on character writing. In early Greek literature, characters were described as generic types. In the fourth century, Theophrastus devised a new method, presenting highly realistic and detailed literary portraits of individuals. The influence of Theophrastus' technique can be traced through the works of later Peripatetics into the writings of Roman satirists and then into medieval literature. In seventeenth-century England and France, Theophrastus' *Characters* were the inspiration for a new wave of interest in character writing. Works by Joseph Hall, Sir Thomas Overbury, John Earle, Samuel Butler and Jean de La Bruyère all built on Theophrastus' *Characters* as the foundational study of character and behaviour. The tradition gathered momentum and was continued in later centuries by such esteemed writers as Alexander Pope, William Thackeray, Charles Dickens and George Eliot. Despite many imitations, Theophrastus' character portraits are still regarded by some as the archetype of brevity and wit: "much imitated, never bettered".[20]

At the heart of this book is a detailed study of the purpose of the *Characters*. Chapter 3 discusses the role of comedy. In particular, it examines Theophrastus' definition of a comic jest as a 'concealed rebuke for error'. This chapter also explores the influence that Theophrastus' teaching had on the comic theatre of Athens. Theophrastus' influence on Menander, who was initially a student at the Peripatos and later became one of the foremost comic playwrights of the time, can clearly be seen in Menander's surviving plays. Previous scholarship has hinted at possible links with comedy.[21] Chapter 3 draws these threads of scholarship together and adds new contributions on Theophrastus' definition of comedy, the purpose of that comedy and its effect on an audience.

Chapter 4 explores the similarities between the *Characters* and Aristotle's ethical philosophy and it argues that Theophrastus' approach is different, innovative and more effective in important ways. Indeed, not all scholars agree that the *Characters* has an ethical dimension.[22] I agree with Lane Fox, Pasquali and Diggle, all of whom have suggested that, in combining ethics with comedy, the *Characters* represents an entirely new genre.[23] I take this suggestion further by explaining *how* comedy and ethics are combined to great effect, *why* Theophrastus chooses only to portray negative behavioural attributes and *how* the *Characters* can be read as a guide to appropriate social conduct. Chapter 4 includes three case-studies of core social values, including friendship, hospitality and shame. These case-studies illustrate the value of the *Characters* for our understanding of social ethics in fourth-century Athens.

Chapter 5 offers a defence of Theophrastus' style of writing in the *Characters*. In my view, Theophrastus' style is quite deliberate and has several merits, including simplicity, clarity, brevity and compactness. Chapter 5 also explores how Theophrastus may have presented his character portraits to an audience and how character portraits were incorporated into rhetorical display-pieces. In a surviving example of a thesis arguing against marriage, Theophrastus presents a character portrait of the 'typical wife', who is as lively, amusing, exaggerated and memorable as any of the male character types he presents in the *Characters*. In Chapter 5, I demonstrate how this character portrait forms the linchpin for the rhetorical argument against marriage.

The last four decades have seen important developments in scholarship on Theophrastus and the compilation of vital source material. In 1979, an international undertaking known as Project Theophrastus was founded to collect, edit and translate source material on Theophrastus. This culminated in the publication of two sourcebooks entitled *Theophrastus of Eresus: Sources for His Life, Writings, Thought and Influence* (1992). Following this, members of the Project turned to producing companion publications in the *Rutgers University Studies in Classical Humanities* series. These publications discuss Theophrastus' life and work, as well as major fields of study to which Theophrastus contributed, including physics, metaphysics, ethics, religion, rhetoric, psychology and biology. It is now an opportune time to reassess the *Characters* in light of what has emerged about Theophrastus' contributions to comedy, ethics and rhetoric.

Fortenbaugh's work on Theophrastus deserves special mention. As the preeminent scholar on Theophrastus, Fortenbaugh has produced important commentaries (especially on ethics[24] and rhetoric[25]) as well as many articles on comic character, laughter, behavioural regularities, fate and character, rhetoric and delivery.[26] Fortenbaugh's scholarship has shaped an entirely new outlook on Theophrastus as a philosopher and his work is referred to many times throughout this book. Importantly, the work initiated by Fortenbaugh is ongoing. Scholars are now examining the contributions made by Theophrastus' colleagues, students and successors. Further commentaries on Theophrastus' scientific works are forthcoming.[27] The expanding interest in Theophrastus and the Peripatetics suggests that this subject will continue to be of interest in the decades to follow.

At this point in time, scholarship on Theophrastus is at an exciting crossroads. Previously, Theophrastus was either unknown or largely overshadowed by Aristotle, rather than being awarded credit as a significant and innovative thinker in his own right.[28] Now, there is greater recognition of Theophrastus' unique contribution as a philosopher and as director of the philosophical school.[29] In turn, this has important ramifications for interpreting Theophrastus' *Characters*. The *Characters* can no longer be dismissed as a curiously lop-sided offshoot of Aristotle's ethical philosophy or as the comic jottings of an inferior philosophical mind. It is an innovative, vibrant and highly influential work that makes its own unique contribution to the fields of ethics, comedy and rhetoric.

In 2007, Millett published his detailed and scholarly study of the *Characters*.[30] Underlying Millett's book is a concern to rescue the *Characters* from becoming "footnote-fodder for studies of 'everyday life' in Athens".[31] Millett reassesses Theophrastus' *Characters* through the lens of three modern works: George Eliot's *Impressions of Theophrastus Such* (1879), Horden and Purcell's work *The Corrupting Sea* (2000), and Diggle's text of the *Characters* (2004). Millett's book deals with many questions of historical interest, such as the effect of Theophrastus' status as a non-Athenian on his leadership of the philosophical school. Millett's analysis of how we can construct a system of etiquette from the *Characters* (chapters 8 and 9) is particularly insightful.

Since the publication of Millett's book in 2007, there have been several important developments. Firstly, there is Fortenbaugh's important commentary on Theophrastus' ethical writings (2011), which has a direct bearing on the *Characters* as an ethical work. Secondly, there is Baltussen's recent work on the Peripatetic philosophers (2016), which points out that differences of opinion and innovation were part and parcel of the school's method. Thirdly, there is growing support for the view that the Peripatos had an influence on Athenian comedy, as is evident from recent work by Casanova (2013). This book engages with these recent developments to provide a new, clearer and up-to-date analysis of the purpose and influence of the *Characters*.

In short, this book builds on the latest developments in scholarship, applying recent findings to a new reading of the *Characters*. It sets out key background information on Theophrastus' life, works and influence, and it seeks to resolve critical questions about the work's purpose in a clear and understandable manner. It argues that Theophrastus' *Characters* represents a new and unique genre, masterfully combining comedic presentation with ethical purpose. In creating his character portraits, Theophrastus expanded and innovated upon Aristotle's ethical theory, connecting the abstract and philosophical study of ethics with the everyday practicalities of life and social interaction.

Notes

1 Baltussen 2016: 8.
2 Diggle 2004: 29.
3 See Habicht 1997: 36–66. Also Green 1990: 36–51.
4 Green 1990: 70.
5 Scholars in favour of an ethical orientation include Petersen 1859: 56–118, Navarre 1964: intro., Regenbogen 1940: 1500–11, Steinmetz 1959, Fortenbaugh 2011: 138. For arguments against see Ussher 1960: 3–4, Diggle 2004: 12, Jebb-Sandys 10–17 and Furley 1953.
6 On the comic aspects of the *Characters* see Ast (1816), Jebb-Sandys at 17, Edmonds 1953: 6, and Vellacott 1967: 9. Also Ussher 1960: 5–6, Fortenbaugh 2003b and Rostagni 1920.

7 Immisch (1923) is the chief proponent of this view. Also see Gordon 1912: 54–6, Furley 1953, Trenkner 1958: 148, Matelli 1989: 329ff and Fortenbaugh 2003a.
8 See Anderson 1970: xiv – xv; also Green 1990: 68.
9 For an overview of the debate see Diggle 2004: 12–16.
10 See Baltussen 2016: 7.
11 See Fortenbaugh 2011: 739ff.
12 MacIntyre 1998: 38.
13 MacIntyre 1998: 43.
14 On this 'resonance' see Lane Fox 1996: 128 and Dover 1974: 2. Also Millett 2007: 42–3.
15 Bobrick 1991: preface. Several papyrus fragments from the first to third centuries CE contain portions of the *Characters*: see Diggle 2004: 37, 38, 50. There are three key manuscripts: Paris manuscripts A (Paris, Bibliothèque Nationale, gr. 2977; no. 44 Wilson) and B (gr. 1983; no. 40 Wilson) from the tenth to eleventh centuries, and the Vatican manuscript V (Biblioteca Apostolica Vaticana, Vat. gr. 110; no. 61 Wilson) from the thirteenth century: see Diggle 2004: 43–9. The manuscripts are in a poor state and centuries of scholarship have been devoted to correcting, amending and reconstructing the Greek text. For further discussion see Wilson 1962.
16 See Diggle 2004: 1–57, and Rusten and Cunningham 2002: 5–39. A full list of editions may be found in Diggle 2004: 524–5. For the scholar, in particular, see the editions of Diels (1909), Immisch (1923) and Navarre (1964).
17 For reviews of Diggle's edition see Worman 2007 and Parker 2006.
18 See TS; and Millett 2007.
19 See Gordon 1912: 49–86, Boyce 1967 and Smeed 1985.
20 Ussher 1960: 3.
21 See Rostagni 1920, Ussher 1960: 4–6, Ussher 1977, Hunter 1985: 148–51, Lane Fox 1996: 140, and Fortenbaugh 2003b.
22 See Furley 1953: 59–60, and Jebb-Sandys: 11–17.
23 See Lane Fox 1996: 139, Pasquali 1918: 77, Diggle 2004: 9 and Jebb-Sandys: 16–17.
24 See Fortenbaugh 2011.
25 Fortenbaugh 2005.
26 Many of these articles have now been translated and collated and appear in Fortenbaugh's 2003 volume cited as TS.
27 See Baltussen and Huby (forthcoming) and Schorn (forthcoming).
28 See Mejer 1998: 5, also Baltussen 2016: esp. at 109 and Sorabji 1998: esp. at 204, 220.
29 FHSG: 1–2.
30 See the review of Millett's book by Scarborough 2009.
31 Millett 2007: 46.

References

Anderson, W. 1970. *Theophrastus: The Character Sketches* (Kent, OH: Kent State University Press).
Ast, D. F. 1816. *Theophrasti Characteres* (Leipzig: Teubner).
Baltussen, H. 2016. *The Peripatetics: Aristotle's Heirs 322 BCE–200 CE* (London: Routledge).
Baltussen, H. and P. M. Huby (eds). Forthcoming. *Theophrastus of Eresus: Sources for His Life, Writings, Thought and Influence*. Commentary Vol. 3.1.1 (Huby): Metaphysics. Vol. 3.1.2 (Baltussen): Fragments in Physical Doxography (Texts 225–245) (Leiden: E.J. Brill).
Bobrick, E. A. 1991. *Theophrastus' Characters* (Bryn Mawr: Bryn Mawr Commentaries).
Boyce, B. 1967. *The Theophrastan Character in England to 1642* (London: Frank Cass & Co.).

Casanova, A. 2013. 'Menander and the Peripatos: New Insights into an Old Question'. In A. H. Sommerstein (ed.) *Menander in Contexts* (New York: Routledge): 137–151.

Diels, H. (ed.) 1909. *Theophrastus, Characters* (Oxford: Oxford University Press).

Diggle, J. 2004. *Theophrastus Characters*. Cambridge Classical Texts and Commentaries 43 (Cambridge: Cambridge University Press).

Dover, K. J. 1974. *Greek Popular Morality in the Time of Plato and Aristotle* (Oxford: Basil Blackwell).

Edmonds, J. M. (ed.) 1953. *The Characters of Theophrastus* (London: William Heinemann).

Fortenbaugh, W. W. 2003a. 'Theophrastus, the Characters and Rhetoric' in TS: 224–243.

Fortenbaugh, W. W. 2003b. 'Theophrastus on Comic Character' in TS: 295–306.

Fortenbaugh, W. W. 2005. *Theophrastus of Eresus: Sources for His Life, Writings, Thought and Influence*. Commentary Volume 8: Sources on Rhetoric and Poetics (Texts 666–713). (Leiden: E. J. Brill).

Fortenbaugh, W. W. 2011. *Theophrastus of Eresus*. Commentary Volume 6.1. Sources on Ethics (Leiden: E. J. Brill).

Furley, D. J. 1953. 'The Purpose of Theophrastus' *Characters*', SO 30.1: 56–60.

Gordon, G. S. 1912. *English Literature and the Classics* (New York: Russell and Russell).

Green, P. 1990. *Alexander to Actium: The Historical Evolution of the Hellenistic Age* (Berkeley and Los Angeles: University of California Press).

Habicht, C. 1997. *Athens from Alexander to Antony* (Cambridge, MA: Harvard University Press).

Hunter, R. L. 1985. *The New Comedy of Greece and Rome* (Cambridge: Cambridge University Press).

Immisch, O. 1923. *Theophrasti Characteres* (Leipzig: Teubner).

Lane Fox, R. 1996. 'Theophrastus' Characters and the Historian', *PCPhS* 42: 127–170.

MacIntyre, A. 1998. *A Short History of Ethics: A History of Moral Philosophy from the Homeric Age to the 20th Century* (2nd ed.) (London: Routledge).

Matelli, E. 1989. 'Libro e testo nella tradizione dei Caratteri di Teofrasto', *S&C* 13: 329–386.

Mejer, J. 1998. 'A Life in Fragments: I *Vita Theophrasti*'. In *RUSCH* Vol. VIII: 1–28.

Millett, P. 2007. *Theophrastus and His World*. Proceedings of the Cambridge Philological Society Supplementary Volume 33 (Cambridge: Cambridge University Press).

Navarre, O. 1964. *Théophraste Caractères* (3rd ed.) (Paris: Les Belles Lettres).

Parker, R. 2006. 'The Learned Commentator of Theophrastus', *CR* 56.2: 308–311.

Pasquali, G. 1918. 'Sui "Caratteri" di Teofrasto', *RLC* 2: 73–79.

Petersen, E. 1859. *Theophrasti Characteres* (Leipzig: Teubner).

Regenbogen, O. 1940. 'Theophrastos', Realencyclopädie der Altertumswissenchaft Suppl. 7, col. 1354–1562.

Rostagni, A. 1920. 'Sui "Caratteri" di Teofrasto', *RFIC* 48: 417–443.

Rusten, J. and I. C. Cunningham. 2002. *Theophrastus Characters, Herodas Mimes, Sophron and Other Mime Fragments* (Cambridge, MA: Harvard University Press).

Scarborough, J. 2009. [Review of Paul Millett: Theophrastus and His World. Proceedings of the Cambridge Philological Society, Supplement Vol. 33. Cambridge: Cambridge University Press, 2007.], *BMCR* 10.55.

Schorn, S. Forthcoming. *Theophrastus of Eresus: Sources for His Life, Writings, Thought and Influence*. Commentary vol. 6.2: Fragments on Religion (Leiden: E.J. Brill).

Smeed, J. W. 1985. *The Theophrastan 'Character': The History of a Literary Genre* (Oxford: Clarendon Press).

Sorabji, R. 1998. 'Is Theophrastus a Significant Philosopher?'. In *RUSCH* Vol. VIII: 203–221.

Steinmetz, P. 1959. 'Der Zweck der Charaktere Theophrasts', *Annales Universitatis Saraviensis. Philosophie* VIII: 209–246.

Trenkner, S. 1958. *The Greek Novella in the Classical Period* (Cambridge: Cambridge University Press).

Ussher, R. G. 1960. *The Characters of Theophrastus* (London: Macmillan & Co).

Ussher, R. G. 1977. 'Old Comedy and "Character": Some Comments', *G&R* 24.1: 71–79.

Vellacott, P. 1967. *Menander: Plays and Fragments, Theophrastus: The Characters* (Harmondsworth: Penguin).

Wilson, N. G. 1962. 'The Manuscripts of Theophrastus', *Scriptorium* 16.1: 96–102.

Worman, N. 2007. [Review of: James Diggle, 2004, *Theophrastus: Characters*. Cambridge Classical Texts and Commentaries 43. Cambridge: Cambridge University Press.], *CW* 100.4, 470–472.

1   Theophrastus
His life, works and character

The contributions of Theophrastus to ancient philosophy and his significance as member, and later director, of Aristotle's philosophical school are not widely known. This chapter provides an outline of Theophrastus' life, a discussion of aspects of his academic partnership with Aristotle and an analysis of his individual achievements. This is followed by a discussion of Theophrastus' works and a brief discussion of Theophrastus' approach and methodology. An analysis of Theophrastus' own character, as a philosopher, scientist and non-Athenian, forms an important backdrop to our study of the *Characters*.

The life of Theophrastus

Theophrastus led a remarkable life. From relatively obscure beginnings, he studied in Athens under two of the greatest philosophers of the time, Plato and Aristotle. His association with Aristotle took him to Asia Minor and then to the royal Macedonian court where Aristotle tutored Alexander the Great. After Aristotle's death in 322 BCE, Theophrastus took over as head of the Peripatos, a position he maintained for more than three decades. In this role, Theophrastus weathered periods of political instability and prosecutions against foreign philosophers, steadfastly furthering his research into diverse subjects, lecturing in the classroom and managing the school. For this role, and his contribution to philosophy, he was honoured by the people of Athens.

The main source for Theophrastus' life is the account recorded by Diogenes Laertius in his *Lives of the Philosophers* from the third century CE.[1] This account was written more than six hundred years after Theophrastus' birth and, as is typical of biographical material from the ancient world, it presents a mixture of reliable, spurious and fictitious material. Compared with the other lives of the philosophers presented by Diogenes, the *Life of Theophrastus* is also relatively brief.[2] Importantly, however, it does provide details of some of the most important events of Theophrastus' life, a list of titles of his works, and a record of his last will and testament. Combined with three other ancient biographies and various other sources, it is possible to piece together a reasonably reliable picture of Theophrastus' life and career.[3]

Theophrastus was born in Eresus on the island of Lesbos around 371 BCE.[4] His birth name was Tyrtamus, a name indicating that he was 'fourth', perhaps the fourth child, or perhaps that he was born on the fourth day of a month or festival.[5] He was the son of Melantas, a wool-worker.[6] After studying under a local philosopher named Alcippus, it is likely that he moved to Athens to pursue an education in Plato's Academy,[7] where he would have studied under Plato and alongside noteworthy figures such as Speusippus and Xenocrates.[8] It was probably at the Academy that he first met Aristotle.[9] Although Aristotle was approximately fourteen years senior in age, the two men forged a strong and enduring intellectual partnership. Aristotle gave Tyrtamus a new name as a tribute to his eloquence.[10] The name was Theophrastus, which means literally, "he who expresses himself like a god".[11]

After Plato's death in 347 BCE, a group of philosophers and students formerly of the Academy left Athens and gathered in Assos, a town opposite the island of Lesbos on the coast of Asia Minor.[12] Theophrastus and Aristotle were among this group. Between 347 and 344/3 BCE, Aristotle conducted various scientific studies in and around the region of Assos,[13] exploring the coastal regions of Asia Minor as well as the island of Lesbos.[14] Theophrastus' intimate knowledge of this region as his birthplace may well have proven useful for Aristotle's studies.[15] In turn, Theophrastus would have witnessed Aristotle's scientific methodology and his approach to data collection and classification. Aristotle's scientific work from this period ultimately culminated in his impressive treatises on biology, including the *History of Animals*.[16]

Aristotle was invited to the royal court of Philip II in Macedonia in 343/2 BCE where he is said to have tutored the young Alexander the Great.[17] It is quite likely that Theophrastus accompanied Aristotle to the Macedonian court and remained there with him for the following eight years.[18] Ancient sources report that Alexander's father supported Aristotle by financing his research and that he also honoured Theophrastus:

> Philip the Macedonian not only was said to be skilled in warfare and a forceful speaker, but he also used to value education very highly. At any rate, by supplying Aristotle with wealth beyond need, he was responsible for much of (Aristotle's) wide experience and therefore also for his knowledge of animals. . . . And he (Philip) also honoured Plato and Theophrastus.[19]

Aristotle's and Theophrastus' connections with Macedon were sustained in later life and were a subject of some controversy.[20] In particular, the sources indicate that there was a connection between Theophrastus and Cassander, who later became king of Macedonia.[21]

Aristotle and Theophrastus returned to Athens in 335 BCE.[22] As a non-Athenian residing in Athens (a *metic*), Aristotle was not permitted to purchase land inside the city of Athens.[23] Instead, Aristotle was permitted to use a parcel of public land located just outside the city.[24] This site was known as the grove of Apollo Lyceus and it contained shrines to Apollo and the Muses.[25] On this site, Aristotle informally established a philosophical school and began teaching. The school came to be known as the Peripatos, so named because of Aristotle's 'peripatetic' habit of walking up and down the covered colonnade while discussing philosophy.[26] The buildings on the property included shrines, as well as porticoes, a library and an altar.[27] The school was dedicated to the accurate observation, classification, and study of nature and it offered a comprehensive curriculum incorporating all of the known sciences.[28] During this time, Theophrastus wrote treatises and lectured at the Peripatos, gaining a reputation for his flair, wit and lively method of delivery.[29] Aristotle is said to have commented on Theophrastus' extraordinary wit and cleverness by comparing him with Callisthenes, saying that Theophrastus "needed a bridle" while Callisthenes needed "a goad".[30]

In 323 BCE, Alexander the Great died and a surge of anti-Macedonian sentiment engulfed Athens.[31] Aristotle, who was viewed as having pro-Macedonian sympathies, left the city and withdrew to Chalcis on the island of Euboea.[32] Shortly after, at sixty-two years of age, he became sick and feeble. A company of Aristotle's followers gathered to wait for him to nominate a successor as new head of the Peripatos.[33] The two candidates for the position were Theophrastus of Lesbos and Eudemus from Rhodes.[34] Aristotle devised a tactful method to choose his preferred successor. He tasted two glasses of wine (one from Rhodes and one from Lesbos) and then stated his preference for the wine from Lesbos saying: "[b]oth are exceedingly good, but the Lesbian is more pleasant."[35] Thus, when Aristotle died shortly after in 322 BCE, Theophrastus succeeded him as head of the Peripatos.

Aristotle's last will and testament indicates that Theophrastus and Aristotle had a close and familial relationship. Theophrastus is named as one of the trustees of Aristotle's property and specifically as guardian of Aristotle's son Nicomachus and his daughter Pythias.[36] Other sources describe how Theophrastus raised Aristotle's son Nicomachus in his house[37] and endeavoured to teach him philosophy:

> (Theophrastus) said to Nicomachus, the son of Aristotle, who was idle in doing philosophy, that it was a good thing not only to be the heir of his paternal property, but also of that man's habits.[38]

In his will, Aristotle explicitly gave permission for his daughter to be married to Theophrastus[39] but there is no evidence that Theophrastus ever married.[40]

As the new head of the Peripatos, Theophrastus proved to be an outstanding successor. Under Theophrastus' leadership, the school grew as a preeminent teaching institution with an impressive number of students and a far-reaching reputation. Diogenes reports that two thousand pupils studied under Theophrastus[41] and this popularity reportedly provoked envy from competing philosophical schools. Zeno, the founder of the Stoic school, apparently remarked, "his chorus is larger, but mine is more harmonious."[42] Well-known figures attended the school, including Aristotle's son Nicomachus, the comic playwright Menander, Erasistratus the physician, Bion of Borysthenes and Demetrius of Phalerum.[43] Even Theophrastus' slave Pompylus is said to have been a philosopher.[44] The popularity of the Peripatos at this time may also have been due in large part to Theophrastus' exuberant teaching style:

> Hermippus says that Theophrastus used to arrive punctually at the Peripatos, looking splendid and all decked out. Then sitting down, he (used to) present his lecture, refraining from no movement nor any gesture.[45]

The period from 317–307 BCE was a politically turbulent time in Athens and this directly affected the Peripatos, which was viewed as having Macedonian connections and sympathies.[46] In 317 BCE, shortly after the city of Athens came under the Macedonian control of the regent Cassander, Theophrastus was prosecuted by Agnonides,[47] an outspoken anti-Macedonian.[48] The charge was alleged impiety (a typical charge brought against philosophers in ancient Athens).[49] In this case, the prosecutors and their allies and supporters were democrats and ardent opponents of Cassander and his father Antipater, which suggests that the allegation was motivated by political interests.[50] Demetrius of Phalerum, who was Theophrastus' former student[51] as well as Cassander's regent in Athens at this time,[52] helped Theophrastus to evade the charge and Agnonides narrowly escaped a fine.[53]

During this period, Demetrius of Phalerum also assisted Theophrastus to acquire ownership over the grounds on which the Peripatos was situated, thereby consolidating the school's future and, in effect, establishing Theophrastus as the trustee of the school.[54] This was an unprecedented property transfer.[55] Theophrastus, like Aristotle, was a non-Athenian. As such, he was ordinarily barred from owning property in Athens. Relying on the patronage of Demetrius of Phalerum, Theophrastus was able to acquire the land as private property for the specific purpose of operating the philosophical school.[56] This acquisition of land formalised the Peripatetic school in a legal and institutional sense with Theophrastus at its head.[57] It also guaranteed the future of the Peripatos, which became a permanent and privately owned entity that could be transferred by succession from one head to another.[58]

The transfer of the school to Theophrastus provoked further hostility and a second prosecution was launched in 307 BCE.[59] The prosecutor was Sophocles of Sunium, the son of Amphiclides, who proposed a law forbidding the establishment of a philosophical school without explicit permission from the Athenian Assembly and Council. The proposed penalty for failure to seek permission was death.[60] Once again, the prosecution appears to have been fuelled by a perception of the Peripatos as anti-democratic and pro-Macedonian, combined with resentment about the unprecedented nature of the property transfer.[61] Demetrius of Phalerum had by this time been expelled from the city of Athens and could offer no assistance.[62] Theophrastus and many other philosophers were required to leave Athens but this expulsion was relatively short lived.[63] The philosophers were able to return a year later after the proposal was challenged.[64] Sophocles was prosecuted by Philon, a pupil of Theophrastus, and he was convicted. The law was then repealed and Sophocles received a hefty fine (five talents).[65] Diogenes cites this episode as proof of the respect that the Athenians had for Theophrastus.[66]

Despite the many political upheavals surrounding the Peripatos, Theophrastus' stewardship of the philosophical school lasted thirty-six years, a period almost three times longer than that of Aristotle's leadership. Theophrastus remained in Athens and his reputation as a philosopher reached as far as Egypt. He was even sent for by Ptolemy, the ruler of Egypt, but he declined the offer.[67] Theophrastus is described by Diogenes in superlative terms, as a "very intelligent and industrious man"[68] and as "ever ready to do a kindness and a lover of words".[69] The Epicureans described him as diligently committed to his philosophical studies and ignorant of "the affairs of monarchs".[70] Some of Theophrastus' favourite sayings were reportedly the saying that "time is a costly expenditure" and that one should more readily "trust in an unbridled horse than in disorganized speech".[71]

As an elderly man, Theophrastus was partially crippled and was carried around in a litter.[72] Even so, he remained dedicated to his scholarly activities. A brief cessation from work appears to have brought on an illness.[73] Theophrastus died in Athens c. 287 BCE, at the age of eighty-five.[74] According to Diogenes, his final words were that "life is short" and that the pursuit of glory is "profitless".[75] He then added: "farewell, and either forsake my teaching – for there is much labor – or champion it well – for the glory is great." [76] The Athenians honoured Theophrastus by escorting his funeral bier on foot.[77]

The last will and testament of Theophrastus is a particularly revealing document.[78] In the course of the political tumult and anti-Macedonian protests that disturbed Athens in 288/7 BCE, parts of the Peripatos had evidently suffered damage.[79] In his will, Theophrastus prioritises precise and detailed instructions for repairs to be made so as to preserve the legacy of Aristotle, as well as to restore and complete the sacred shrine, commemorative statues of Aristotle and Nicomachus, altar and sanctuary.[80] As for the garden and estate of the Peripatos, Theophrastus is touchingly concerned that his ten legatees hold the property in common as a philosophical community with a shared love of learning.[81] This is evident from the following instructions in his will:

> The garden and the walk and all the dwellings next to the garden I give to those of (my) friends listed below who wish at any time to study and to philosophize together in them – since it is not possible for all men to be always in residence – (on the condition that) they neither alienate (them) nor anyone appropriate (them) for his own private use, but rather that they possess (them) in common, as if a shrine, and that in matters of mutual concern they use (them) in a familiar and friendly manner, just as is fitting and just.[82]

The extent of Theophrastus' personal wealth is also apparent from his will, with mention of properties at Stagira and Eresus, large sums of money and ten slaves.[83] Theophrastus' library (which included Aristotle's books) was left to his pupil Neleus.[84] As for the instructions for his own burial, they are exceedingly brief and modest:

> Bury me wherever seems to be especially suitable in the garden, doing nothing excessive concerning the burial nor concerning the monument.[85]

The picture of Theophrastus that emerges from the source material is a man from a modest and non-Athenian background with a remarkable wit and intellect and a deep love of scientific and philosophical inquiry. Theophrastus clearly had a voracious appetite for knowledge, as well as being an engaging and flamboyant lecturer, a well-connected individual with influential friends and allies, an outstanding leader of the Peripatos, and a well-known member of the Athenian community who was respected by the Athenians. Apart from leading the Peripatos into its most significant and outstanding period of scholarship, Theophrastus' will indicates the primacy of his philosophical values. Above all else, he is concerned to pass the torch of philosophical enquiry to worthy successors. Theophrastus' immediate successor was Strato of Lampsacus, who remained head of the school for a further eighteen years.[86]

Theophrastus' works

Theophrastus was a remarkable polymath who produced over two hundred works of varying lengths on an astonishingly diverse range of subjects. In his will, Theophrastus bequeathed this vast corpus of works to his pupil, Neleus of Scepsis, after which time the books suffered neglect and damage, having been placed in the hands of 'unaspiring' and 'ordinary' men.[87] It is unfortunate that only the titles of the majority of Theophrastus' works remain.[88] The titles include works on logic, metaphysics, physics, psychology, human physiology, zoology, botany, ethics, religion, politics, rhetoric, poetics and music.[89]

Two of Theophrastus' extant works, entitled *Investigations into Plants* and *Explanations for Plants*, are particularly significant. These works established Theophrastus' reputation as the founding father of botanical science. They are equivalent in scale, and complementary to, Aristotle's zoological studies,[90] and they indicate that Theophrastus was Aristotle's equal in the realm of scientific research and classification.[91] Apart from these botanical works, there are two shorter treatises: one investigating principles of nature (*Metaphysics*) and one evaluating various theories about the senses (*On the Senses*). A number of minor scientific treatises are also extant, including works on human physiology (*On Sweat, On Signs of Fatigue*) and works on various natural phenomena (*On Fire, On Odours, On Weather Signs* and *On Fish*).[92] The surviving scientific works of Theophrastus are indicative of one of the overarching objectives of the Peripatos, which was to classify and study a wide range of natural phenomena.[93]

The *Characters* is a particularly distinctive work because of its unique subject and its informal style. As a result, some have suggested that Theophrastus wrote the work mainly for his own amusement and that the work was published later by his students or friends.[94] This suggestion seems too much influenced by the later tradition of character writing, especially the character portraits written by Sir Thomas Overbury, which were published posthumously by Overbury's friends.[95] Another possibility is that the character portraits were intended to be presented to a public audience, although we cannot assume that lectures within the Peripatos were always very formal, or that Theophrastus only gave public lectures on light-hearted and informal topics. In a letter written to a fellow-Peripatetic,

Theophrastus hints that public audiences could be just as demanding as others, saying that "it is not easy to get a public assembly . . . such as one would like" and that "public readings lead to revisions".[96] Instead, Fortenbaugh has suggested that Theophrastus wrote the *Characters* for use both within and outside of the Peripatos.[97] This seems more likely given that the combination of ethics and comedy in the *Characters* could appeal to different types of audiences.

The text of the *Characters*

In the catalogue of works preserved by Diogenes, Theophrastus' *Characters* are cited twice, first as the "ethikoi characteres" and second as the "characteres ethikoi".[98] This repetition is curious because only one book of *Characters* has survived. As Diggle has pointed out, Diogenes' list of works is made up of several lists and this may explain the repetition.[99] Other possibilities are that the work was known by both titles, or that there were different copies of the work in circulation, bearing different titles.[100]

The title of the work itself requires consideration. The literal meaning of the noun '*characteres*' is 'something cut or marked', such as the imprint or stamp on a coin or seal, but metaphorically the noun refers to a 'distinctive mark' or 'feature' and is used to refer to an individual's distinctive physical features, style of speech or style of writing.[101] In the context of this work, '*characteres*' means 'distinctive marks or features'.[102] Importantly, the adjective '*ethikos*' means 'expressive of moral character' rather than 'ethical' in the philosophical sense.[103] Theophrastus is generally (although not universally) accepted to be the author of the work.[104]

The realistic setting of the *Characters* is one of the most distinctive features of the work.[105] The setting is urban Athens[106] and it betrays Theophrastus' long and intimate acquaintance with the city and its residents. Aside from a few variations, the setting is generally consistent throughout the work; and there is no difficulty in assuming that most of the venues are Athenian, whether they involve the marketplace, theatre, law courts or assembly.[107]

Estimates for the date of the work range from the 330s to 319 BCE,[108] with some preference for a date around 319 BCE.[109] One of the difficulties with arriving at a precise date is that although the text refers to particular historical events and political figures,[110] different character portraits are set during different political eras. Furthermore, references to historical events are made by characters that are inclined to boast, exaggerate and misrepresent information.[111] Diggle concludes that it is impossible to settle on a fixed date and only commits to a date in the later part of the fourth century.[112] It has also been suggested that the work was composed over an extended period[113] and published after Theophrastus' death.[114]

The text of the *Characters* clearly betrays evidence of interference from later authors. In particular, a twenty-five-line prologue has been added to the beginning of the work.[115] This prologue describes Theophrastus as ninety-nine years of age[116] and sets the *Characters* in the context of a dialogue with a certain Polycles about the natures of different types of men. The prologue indicates that the work will describe noble and ignoble character types but, as we know, the portraits are of negative types only.[117] Apart from the prologue, concluding remarks or epilogues appear after nine of the thirty character portraits.[118] These epilogues introduce a moralising tone that is foreign to the rest of the work.[119]

The definitions that introduce each character type are also of doubtful authenticity as many of them are vague, loosely phrased or do not match the description of the character type that follows.[120] On the one hand, it was typical of Peripatetic writing to begin with a definition and to assess the appropriateness of the definition as analysis proceeded.[121] On the other hand, Theophrastus wrote a number of works on definitions and criticised the accuracy of definitions contained in the writings of his contemporaries.[122] It is hard to believe that Theophrastus would have been satisfied with the definitions in the *Characters*, many of which are banal or inadequate.[123] Diggle argues forcefully that we must either accept or reject the definitions as a whole and, following Diggle, we will adopt the latter approach.[124] Once we have removed the definitions, prologue and epilogues, we are left with the core of the text: thirty short descriptions of character types, each approximately twenty-five to thirty lines in length, and each cataloguing examples of conduct and speech.[125]

Theophrastus' character as philosopher, scientist and non-Athenian

There are three dimensions of Theophrastus' character that help us to understand his point of view in writing the *Characters*: namely, Theophrastus as philosopher, scientist and non-Athenian resident or *metic*. As a philosopher, Theophrastus had a very close association and intellectual partnership with Aristotle. The research interests of the two men often overlapped and their studies were often complementary. This is reflected in the ancient sources, which often mention the works of both philosophers in the same breath. Strabo, Plutarch and Porphyry, for example, all refer to the "books of Aristotle and Theophrastus" as part of the same collection.[126] The ancient sources also position Theophrastus alongside the most esteemed philosophical figures of the time, including Aristotle, Plato, Socrates, Zeno, Epicurus and Diogenes the Cynic.[127]

Based on the views expressed in ancient sources, can we assess the extent to which Theophrastus was an original thinker? The source material presents a spectrum of opinions. Simplicius represents one extreme and describes Theophrastus as a follower of Aristotle "in almost everything".[128] Boethius represents the opposite extreme, stating that it is typical of Theophrastus to touch lightly upon topics that Aristotle had already dealt with and diligently pursue topics that had not been covered.[129] Quintilian represents the middle ground. In the context of discussing rhetoric, he states that on some topics, Theophrastus follows Aristotle's authority but that, otherwise, Theophrastus is "accustomed fearlessly to dissent from him".[130] Cicero defends Theophrastus based on his style, saying that although Theophrastus might deal with the same topics as Aristotle, he is still enjoyable to read.[131]

An analysis of Theophrastus' extant works suggests that the extent to which Theophrastus diverges from Aristotle depends on the topic in question.[132] At times,

Theophrastus is clearly aligned with Aristotle and furthers his work or deals with related topics, as in the subject of ethics.[133] At other times, Theophrastus is both innovative and original (such as his *Metaphysics* and his work *On Delivery*).[134] Sometimes there is fundamental disagreement between the two (for example, Theophrastus' opposition to animal sacrifice).[135] Where Theophrastus disagrees with Aristotle, or points out difficulties with his theories, he does not always provide a new theory of his own, but this was not necessarily his aim, and it is in keeping with the general approach of the Peripatetics.[136] The aim of the Peripatos was to conduct broad and constructive philosophical inquiries, not to adopt single, definitive views on each topic.[137] As Baltussen has observed, Theophrastus' particular strength was in meticulously describing multiple explanations for natural phenomena, rather than generating overarching theories to explain phenomena.[138]

In evaluating Theophrastus' alignment with, or departure from, Aristotelian ideas, it is also important to recognise that discussion and disagreement were an integral part of the academic approach of the Peripatetic school. The primary objective of the school was "the collection and interpretation of information in every field, and . . . the raising and the attempted resolution of theoretical difficulties".[139] To achieve this objective, the Peripatetic method involved establishing a line of enquiry, amassing all the relevant evidence, examining the views of others in line with that evidence, and agreeing or disagreeing openly by showing weaknesses in logic and reasoning.[140] This methodology applied to the whole range of studies covered by the school, whether botany, metaphysics, ethics, zoology, physics, politics or rhetoric. Ancient sources provide some insight into the rigorous methodology that the teachers applied in the classroom:

> Plato, Pythagoras, Aristotle and Theophrastus, who did indeed preside over philosophy, appeared inclined to anger toward those who esteemed their studies lightly, yet they did not pour forth a fountain of words so ungrudgingly, but set certain principles and seeds before their students and then indeed demanded back much more than what they laid down.[141]

The result was not necessarily a single, consistent opinion or a definitive theory but the opening up of new lines of enquiry.[142]

This leads us to consider Theophrastus' methodology as a scientist. A careful reading of the full range of Theophrastus' extant scientific works reveals some important aspects of Theophrastus' methodology that can also be observed in the *Characters*. Although it is not a scientific work, the *Characters* clearly contains traces of Peripatetic methodology that were applied across different disciplines.[143]

One very distinctive feature of Theophrastus' scientific writings, and of the approach of the Peripatetics in general, is the emphasis on *classification and differentiation*.[144] Theophrastus regarded the primary task of science as one that involved grouping living organisms according to certain shared attributes:

> In general, scientific knowledge involves understanding what is the same in many things, whether described as things in common or generally, or in some particular way according to each.[145]

In *Investigations into Plants*, for example, Theophrastus demonstrates this technique by classifying plants in broad categories, according to whether they are trees, shrubs or herbs.[146] Theophrastus defines these groups further by noting differences with respect to their component parts, such as leaves, seeds, flowers and fruits.[147] In his work *On Stones*, Theophrastus uses the same method of classification to distinguish between particular types of stones, noting differences in smoothness, solidity and transparency.[148] Precisely the same process of classification underpins the *Characters*.[149] Each individual character portrait is representative of a 'type' or 'group' that can be differentiated by their distinctive appearance, attributes, manner of speech and modes of behaviour. These types belong to larger classificatory groups that share common defects or vices such as garrulity, avariciousness and grossness.[150] In turn, classification according to type is relevant to ethics, comedy and rhetoric, but it has particular implications for the development and portrayal of stock character types in Athenian comedy (discussed in Chapter 3).

Theophrastus' interest in *anomalies and peculiarities of nature* is another prominent feature of his scientific works. In his *Explanations for Plants*, Theophrastus conducts an enquiry into unnatural occurrences in plants, including the failure of a plant to produce proper fruit or shoots, at the proper season and from the correct part of the plant.[151] Mutations in the roots or entire plant are discussed,[152] as well as other forms of disease.[153] These anomalies are of interest to Theophrastus as a scientist because they place the normal and natural in stark relief and because, as Theophrastus says, "disease is always a departure from the natural".[154] A similar interest can be observed in Theophrastus' character portraits, in the comic distortion of the behaviour of the characters, and the anomalous and peculiar forms of human behaviour that Theophrastus describes. Just as Theophrastus' study of disease serves to highlight the natural and normal, Theophrastus' study of behavioural deviations serves to highlight and reinforce social norms (discussed further in Chapter 4).

Theophrastus is also fond of analysing phenomena according to the concepts of *excess and deficiency*. In his botanical works, for example, Theophrastus describes the difference between categories of plants as essentially a matter of excess or deficiency in either number or size.[155] Similarly, in his work *On Fire*, Theophrastus discusses the results of excessive oxygenation and fuel consumption.[156] The notions of excess and defect can be observed in the doctrine of the mean that underlies Theophrastus' descriptions of character types, as each type can be viewed as representing either an 'excess' or 'deficiency' relative to a particular virtue (such as the *Obsequious Man*, who is excessively friendly, and the *Self-Centred Man*, who is exceedingly unfriendly).[157]

A wealth of factual material drawn from *practical everyday experience* as well as reports from a wide variety of unspecified sources feature in Theophrastus' scientific treatises.[158] In his treatise *On Stones*, some passages suggest that Theophrastus consulted tradespeople, such as stonemasons, and perhaps observed their activities directly.[159] In Theophrastus' botanical writings, he presents all manner of information, from the technical expertise of joiners and expert artisans[160] to the folklore and popular wisdom of druggists and herb-diggers.[161] The same familiarity with practical tradespeople is evident in the *Characters*. The conduct of the characters takes place against a highly realistic backdrop filled with practical trades and professions including shopkeepers, wool-workers, tanners, hairdressers, courtesans, soldiers, teachers and bath attendants.

Theophrastus' scientific works also demonstrate that he had a *highly analytical mindset* and that he made uncompromising criticisms of the inadequacies of certain theories. Criticism was not for criticism's sake alone (nor was it unwarranted in many instances). In accordance with the Peripatetic method, Theophrastus sought to identify weaknesses in reasoning and to show how these weaknesses undermined the overall proposition.[162] Almost half of Theophrastus' work *On the Senses*, for example, is devoted to criticism (including criticism of the theories of such esteemed thinkers as Empedocles, Democritus and Plato).[163] It is very likely that Theophrastus carried his gift for 'passionless scrutiny'[164] beyond the porticoes of the Peripatos and out into the streets of Athens. Theophrastus' analysis of his fellow Athenians in the *Characters* is highly critical. Theophrastus meticulously observes, records and 'shows up' undesirable character traits and behaviours. Furthermore, Theophrastus' artfully brief and realistic descriptions of the character types reflect his own high standards of economy, accuracy, factual representation and internal consistency.[165]

Lastly, but importantly, there is Theophrastus' appreciation of *the unusual and humorous side of life*. Even amidst his serious scientific observations, there are humorous anecdotes and stories and a manifest delight in the idiosyncrasies of nature. In the midst of discussing the best types of wood for load-bearing purposes in his *Investigations into Plants*, for example, Theophrastus relates an amusing anecdote about a particular attribute of sweet chestnut wood: "it is said that when it is about to split, it makes a noise, so that men are forewarned: this occurred once at Antandros at the baths, and all those present rushed out."[166] On another occasion, Theophrastus relates an amusing story about a shepherd who destroyed a drug-seller's reputation by eating a large quantity of a supposedly toxic herb and suffering no ill effects.[167] The same brand of humour is evident in the *Characters*, in which Theophrastus records examples of idiosyncratic and amusing behaviour.

As a philosopher and scientist, Theophrastus was clearly comfortable writing about a vast array of subjects, from logic, ethics, and the highest principles of metaphysics to honey, fruits and insects that sting. Whatever the subject, there are aspects of his scientific methodology and approach that remain consistent, especially his method of classifying, his preoccupation with the concepts of excess and deficiency, and his interest in peculiarities of nature. It is not surprising then that some have concluded that the *Characters* is a scientific work. Anderson, for example, has suggested that the character portraits "are the field reports of a scientist botanizing in Athens".[168] Trenkner describes the *Characters* as "a scientific, not a literary work".[169] Green writes that it is very tempting to regard the *Characters* as "an attempt to apply the principles of botanical classification to human beings, to typologize men as one would flowers".[170]

Methodological similarities, however, are not sufficient to establish scientific purpose. In the *Characters*, Theophrastus applies his skills in observation and classification to observing a very specific sector of society. For a scientific work, one would expect a broader sample, including women, members of the lower classes and non-Athenians.[171] Nor is the *Characters* a 'scientific' work in the sense that Theophrastus' observations are objective, impartial and without judgement.[172] As we shall see in Chapter 4, Theophrastus' studies of inappropriate social behaviour imply strong views about ethical conduct and appropriate social etiquette. Although the *Characters* reflects the general approach and methodology of the Peripatetic school, the purpose of the work is a separate and more complex question (discussed in Chapters 3 and 4).

The third and final aspect of Theophrastus' character that requires consideration is Theophrastus' social status as a *metic* or alien resident in Athens. As a native of the island of Lesbos, Theophrastus was categorised as an outsider and could never hold the social status of a native Athenian. *Metics* were required to pay a monthly tax for the privilege of residing in the city or else face enslavement, they could not own property in Athens and they had to nominate a citizen-friend to act as patron to enable them to rent property in Athens.[173] The attempt in 307 BCE to ban foreign philosophers from presiding over philosophical schools without explicit government permission was partly an attempt to target Theophrastus and other philosophers as *metics*. Theophrastus is said to have reported that the Athenians referred to *metics* as 'bowl-carriers' since they marched in public processions carrying bowls;[174] and because the *metic* had no freedom of speech, the Athenians could threaten to make a *metic* "more mute than a bowl".[175]

Theophrastus may not have been considered a born and bred Athenian, but he was not the usual *metic* either.[176] He led one of the most prominent philosophical schools of the times and had powerful friends and political connections at the Macedonian court.[177] It was Theophrastus' former student and the leader of Athens, Demetrius of Phalerum, who enabled him to buy the property on which the philosophical school was situated. Theophrastus reportedly dressed well[178] and spoke well,[179] and his will testifies to his extensive wealth, including slaves, money, property inside and outside of Athens, and household possessions.[180] According to Lane Fox, "[Theophrastus'] will reveals ownership of even more slaves than any of his Characters and his style of life as Aristotle's heir was well up to the upper reaches of his upper Characters."[181]

Theophrastus' dual identity as a *metic* and prominent philosopher in Athens may well have given him a unique viewpoint on the Athenians.[182] As an 'outsider', Theophrastus may have been especially well placed to examine the Athenians with a measure of objectivity. He may even have enjoyed turning the tables on the Athenians and transforming his status as an outsider into an advantage as he played the role of both observer and commentator in presenting his character portraits to an audience within, as well as outside of, the Peripatos. At the same time, Theophrastus was a long-term resident of Athens, a member of the wealthier classes and presumably a well-known face in Athenian society.[183] The Athenians called for his return from exile in 306 BCE and paid special honours to him at his funeral. For his part, Theophrastus does not caricature the Athenians with a brutal and disinterested wit but with the good humour stemming from a closeness and familiarity with one's subject.

Given Theophrastus' background, it is also important to consider the sector of society that is targeted in the *Characters*. The setting of the work as well as the activities and lifestyles that are referred to indicate that all of the characters are Athenian citizens.[184] There are no *metics* or foreigners targeted in the character portraits, although foreigners, guest-friends and slaves are frequently mentioned in passing.[185] As for the class of men who form the subject of the work, some belong to the highest social classes, others are citizens of modest property but still slave-owners,[186] and still others belong to less reputable (but not lower-class) professions.[187] In short, the subjects of the *Characters* are all "mature, male citizens of good standing".[188] As to why all of the characters tend to be of mature age,[189] Lane Fox offers a possible answer: "[o]lder men, as comedy recognized, were more set in their ways and therefore more apt for the one-sided types which Theophrastus isolated."[190]

Notes

1   DL 5.36–58 = fr. 1. Textual apparatus in Sollenberger 1985. Discussion in Sollenberger 1992 and Mejer 1998.
2   Mejer 1998: 10.
3   The sources for Theophrastus' life are collated in FHSG: frs. 1–36.
4   On birth date see Mejer 1998: 17.
5   See Sollenberger 1992: 3833–4.
6   On Melantas see Sollenberger 1992: 3805. A wool-worker (fuller) washed cloths and fabrics, particularly cloaks. Fullers are mentioned in the *Characters* (22.8, 30.10) as are cloaks (see 2.3, 5.6, 19.6, 21.8, 26.4 and 27.5).
7   DL 5.36 = fr. 1. Discussed by Sollenberger 1992: 3806–7.
8   See Fortenbaugh and Harmon 2017.
9   Theophrastus may have first met Aristotle in Assos: see Diggle 2004: 2, but the sources suggest that Theophrastus was Plato's student first and then aligned himself with Aristotle: see Mejer 1998: 17–19.
10 DL 5.38 = fr. 1. Also see frs 5A, 5B, 5C and 5D. The Suda says that Aristotle first named him Euphrastus and later Theophrastus (fr. 2).
11 Fortenbaugh says that the story of Theophrastus' name change is "not credible" (Fortenbaugh 2011: 63) and several other scholars have expressed doubts (see Sollenberger 1992: 3834 n. 213) but Sollenberger notes that name changes and nicknames were not uncommon in ancient times (Sollenberger 2000: 3834). In Theophrastus' case, it may have been desirable to adopt a more Athenian-sounding name. Athenian inscriptions indicate that Theophrastus was a relatively common name in the fifth to third centuries BCE: see Sollenberger 1992: 3834 and Millett 2007: 26.
12 Diggle 2004: 2.
13 Grayeff 1974: 30.
14 Furley 1999a: 2.
15 Millett 2007: 53.
16 For discussion of Aristotle's zoological works see Furley 1999b: 27–9.
17 DL 5.4; discussion in Sollenberger 1992: 3818.
18 Sollenberger 1992: 3843.
19 Aelian, *Miscellaneous History* 4.19 = fr. 28.
20 See Sollenberger 1992: 3820–1.
21 DL 5.37 = fr. 1; Suda, *On Theophrastos* = fr. 2.
22 On chronology see Sollenberger 1992: 3843.

23 Mejer 1998: 20.
24 On the exact location of the Peripatos see Millett 2007: 21–2.
25 Grayeff 1974: 38.
26 DL 5.2; discussed in Sollenberger 1992: 3810. It is also referred to as the Lyceum (after the grove of Apollo Lyceus).
27 These are the buildings explicitly mentioned in Theophrastus' will (DL 5.51–53 = fr. 1).
28 Glucker 1998: 312, also Grayeff 1974: 39.
29 Athenaeus, *The Sophists at Dinner* 1.38 21A–B = fr. 12.
30 DL 5.39 = fr. 1, lines 35–38. On the authenticity of this anecdote see Fortenbaugh 2011: 63, Sollenberger 1992: 3835 and Mejer 1998: 9 n.23.
31 See Millett 2007: 130 n. 86.
32 DL 5.36; discussed in Sollenberger 1992: 3810.
33 Aulus Gellius, *Attic Nights* 13.5.1–2 = fr. 8.
34 Aulus Gellius, *Attic Nights* 13.5.3–4 = fr. 8.
35 Aulus Gellius, *Attic Nights* 13.5.9–10 = fr. 8, lines 20–1. Mejer calls this episode a "fancy story" (Mejer 1998: 20) but it does indicate that there was more than one candidate for the position (see Sollenberger 1992: 3811).
36 Aristotle, *Will* in DL 5.12–13 = fr. 19.
37 Aristocles of Messene, fr. 2 Heiland, in Eusebius, *Evangelical Preparation* 15.2.15 = fr. 20.
38 *Gnomologium Vaticanum* no. 330 = fr. 21.
39 Aristotle, *Will* in DL 5.12–13 = fr. 19.
40 There is no wife or child mentioned in Theophrastus' will (as there is in Aristotle's). Aristippus, in a work entitled *On Ancient Luxury*, apparently said that Theophrastus was erotically attracted to Aristotle's son Nicomachus (see DL 5.39 = fr.1; also Suda, *On Theophrastos* = fr. 2).
41 DL 5.37 = fr. 1. Millett assumes that Diogenes' figures are exaggerated (see Millett 2007: 33) as does Diggle 2004: 3 at n.9. Mejer also has doubts: Mejer 1998: 21. Gottschalk's comparison with the numbers of admissions at Trinity College Cambridge is neither relevant nor persuasive: see Gottschalk 1998: 283. It is more likely that the number refers to those who attended Theophrastus' popular lectures: see Sollenberger 1992: 3828.
42 Plutarch, *How One May Be Aware of His Progress in Virtue* 6 78D = fr. 15. On Theophrastus and the Stoics generally see Long 1998.
43 See sources listed at fr. 18.15 (Nicomachus), fr. 18.12 (Menander), fr. 18.8 (Erasistratus), fr. 18.3 (Bion) and fr. 18.5 (Demetrius). On Demetrius' political career and association with the Peripatos see Gottschalk 2000.
44 DL 5.36 (quoting Myronianus of Amastris' first book of *Summary of Historical Parallels*) = fr. 1. A further testament to Theophrastus' popularity is that he apparently attracted students from outside the Peripatos: see Mejer 1998: 9.
45 Athenaeus, *The Sophists at Dinner* 1.38 21A–B = fr. 12.
46 O'Sullivan 2009: 204–5.
47 DL 5.37 = fr. 1.
48 O'Sullivan 2009: 205.
49 See DL 5.37 = fr. 1; discussion in Sollenberger 1992: 3820 and O'Sullivan 2009: 206. On similar allegations of impiety made against Aristotle see Sollenberger 1992: 3819–20. This court case may have been the occasion on which Theophrastus was reportedly lost for words in the Assembly (as reported in Aelian, *Miscellaneous History* 8.12 = fr. 32A).
50 O'Sullivan 2009: 205–6. For a discussion of Theophrastus' own political leanings see Lane Fox 1996: 133–4.
51 Sollenberger 2000: 316.
52 Sollenberger 2000: 313.

53 DL 5.37 = fr. 1.
54 DL 5.39 = fr. 1. Also see Gottschalk 2000: 368 and Grayeff 1974: 50.
55 O'Sullivan 2002: 256.
56 O'Sullivan 2002: 254.
57 Sollenberger 1992: 3823. Also Mejer 1998: 20, n.59.
58 O'Sullivan 2002: 256–7.
59 See O'Sullivan 2002: 260.
60 DL 5.38 = fr. 1.
61 See O'Sullivan 2002: 252–3, Gottschalk 1998: 282–3.
62 On Demetrius' exile see Sollenberger 2000: 318–20.
63 On the effects of the expulsion on the cultural life and economic prosperity of the city see Sollenberger 1992: 3822.
64 See Gottschalk 2000: 375–6.
65 DL 5.38 = fr. 1. For discussion see O'Sullivan 2002: 252, and Millett 2007: 25.
66 DL 5.38 = fr. 1.
67 DL 5.37 = fr. 1.
68 DL 5.36 = fr. 1, line 10.
69 DL 5.37 = fr. 1, lines 12–13. On Diogenes' terms of praise see Sollenberger 1992: 3814.
70 Philodemus, *Notebook on Rhetoric*, P. Herc. 240 fr. 16.3–10 = fr. 27. Discussed by Mejer 1998: 11 and n. 30.
71 DL 5.39–40 = fr. 1, lines 44–5, 41–2.
72 DL 5.41 = fr. 1.
73 DL 5.40 = fr.1. Suda, on *Theophrastos* = fr. 2. Discussed by Mejer 1998: 17 esp. n.49.
74 DL 5.40 = fr. 1; Diggle 2004: 3.
75 Curiously, Diogenes does not record the last words of any of the Peripatetics other than Theophrastus (see Sollenberger 1992: 3841).
76 DL 5.41 = fr. 1, lines 55–7.
77 DL 5.41 = fr. 1.
78 Following careful linguistic analysis, Sollenberger concludes that all four wills preserved by Diogenes in book 5 (including Theophrastus') are authentic: see Sollenberger 1992: 3859–72.
79 Gottschalk presents an alternative view of the Peripatos at this time, suggesting that it was well established with a secure future: Gottschalk 1998: 283.
80 DL 5.51–52 = fr. 1, lines 298–307.
81 See discussion in Sollenberger 1992: 3811–2; 3867.
82 DL 5.52–53 = fr. 1, lines 311–317.
83 DL 5.54–56 = fr. 1. For analysis see Millett 2007: 20–1.
84 Strabo, *Geography* 13.1.54 = fr. 37.
85 DL 5.53–54 = fr. 1, lines 324–6. On the modesty expected of philosophers and the relevant burial laws see O'Sullivan 2009: 199–200.
86 On Strato and the later decline of the Peripatos see Baltussen 2016: 63–5, Sharples 1999: 147–55 and Sharples 1998.
87 Plutarch, *Sulla* 26.1–3 = fr 38. On Neleus see Gottschalk 1998: 291–2. On the later history of the texts see Diggle 2004: 3. The texts were reportedly stored underground, suffered damage, sold to Apellicon of Teos, taken to Rome and copied. It is also possible that Demetrius of Phalerum had made copies of many of Aristotle's and Theophrastus' works: see Mejer 1998: 27.
88 For the list of titles see DL 5.42–51 = fr. 1, lines 68–291.
89 See Mejer 1998: 22ff and Sollenberger 1992: 3852–5.
90 For a discussion of Theophrastus' contribution to botanical science see Fraser 1994: esp. 188. There appears to have been "a deliberate division of labour" with Theophrastus writing on plants and Aristotle writing on animals: see Fortenbaugh and Harmon 2017.

91 On similarities between Aristotle's zoological works and Theophrastus' botanical works see Gotthelf 1988. Also see Wöhrle 1985.

92 For a summary of these works see Ierodiakonou 2016.

93 Glucker 1998: 312.

94 See Lane Fox 1996: 141, also Jebb-Sandys: 16–17.

95 Anderson 1970: xxiii.

96 DL 5.37 (quoting a letter Theophrastus allegedly wrote to Phanias the Peripatetic) = fr. 1, lines 18–21.

97 Fortenbaugh 2011: 740.

98 DL 5.47–8 = fr. 1 at lines 201, 241.

99 See Diggle 2004: 18–19.

100 Fortenbaugh 2005: 88.

101 Diggle 2004: 4.

102 Diggle 2004: 5.

103 See Diggle 2004: 5 n.15, also Fortenbaugh 2011: 138.

104 See Ussher 1960: 3. For a list of doubters see Diggle 2004: 16.

105 For discussion see Rusten and Cunningham 2002: 9; Lane Fox 1996: 129–30; Diggle 2004: 8. Habicht 1997: 122–3.

106 Millett 2007: 54. For references to events and places outside of Athens: see Millett 2007: 54–7.

107 Lane Fox 1996: 129.

108 In fact, there are three dates in question: dramatic date, date of composition and date of publication. These questions are dealt with in detail by Diggle 2004: 27–37.

109 The date of 319 BCE was established by Cichorius (1897): see Diggle 2004: 27–8. See also Rusten and Cunningham 2002: 10–12, Jebb-Sandys at 7, Ussher 1960: 13, Boegehold 1959, and Lane Fox 1996: 134–9.

110 There are historical references pertaining to military service with Alexander the Great (23.3); an invitation from Antipater to visit the province of Macedonia (23.4); a battle against Polyperchon (8.6–7); and the capture of Cassander (8.7).

111 The two character types who refer to historical events are the *Boastful Man* who grossly exaggerates his achievements, and the *Rumour-Monger* who is characterised by his dishonest story-telling.

112 Although Diggle concludes that it is impossible to determine a consistent dramatic date, date of composition or date of publication (Diggle 2004: 36–7), he seems to lean towards a date around 319 BCE (see at 29, 32).

113 Navarre suggests that Theophrastus wrote the *Characters* over an extended period (322–317 BCE): Navarre 1924: xiii. Diggle's conclusion is similar: Diggle 2004: 37 n. 119. See also Lane Fox 1996: 138.

114 See Lane Fox 1996: 141.

115 Diggle 2004: 16. A copy of this prologue may be found in Diggle 2004: 62–3. There are some similarities with the opening lines of Theophrastus' *Metaphysics* (1.1–3) which also posits a basic question, comments on the infinite variety in nature and then announces a starting point for the enquiry.

116 Diogenes says that Theophrastus died at the age of eighty-five: DL 5.40 = fr. 1.

117 Although the possibility of a second book of noble character types has found some support, Diggle firmly dismisses the possibility: see Diggle 2004: 18–19. For a list of scholars who argue in favour of a second book see Diggle 2004: 18 at n. 60. The persistence of the notion of a second book does, I think, indicate a level of discomfort with the perceived 'negativity' of the work. Possible reasons for the focus on negative traits are discussed in Chapter Four.

118 Diggle 2004: 16–17.

119 According to Jebb, these epilogues were added by "someone who could not perceive that the quiet humour of the descriptions was spoilt by hortatory comments": Jebb-Sandys: 18. Also Fortenbaugh 2011: 139.

120 Diggle 2004: 17. Also see Ussher 1960: 7. Those in favour of accepting the defini-
    tions are Navarre 1924: xxv–viii; Steinmetz 1962: 8–16. Fortenbaugh suggests they
    may have been 'working' definitions: Fortenbaugh 2003b: 231.
121 Ackrill 1981: 11.
122 Theophrastus wrote three books on *Definitions* and one book *Concerning Definitions*:
    DL 5.43, at line 96 and 5.45 at line 138. His treatise *On the Senses* roundly criticises
    the inadequate definitions of others: see Baltussen 2000: at 107, 111, 122 and 124.
    Also see Stratton 1917: 58.
123 See for example the circular definition of the *Shabby Profiteer* (30.1) and the descrip-
    tion (not definition) of the *Chatterbox* (3.1).
124 Diggle 2004: 17.
125 Even this core text is peppered with later additions: see Diggle 2004: 17–18. In addi-
    tion, there are many gaps in the text as well as two fragments that are awkwardly
    tacked onto characters five (the *Obsequious Man*) and nineteen (the *Offensive Man*).
126 See Strabo, *Geography* 13.1.54 = fr. 37, Plutarch, *Sulla* 26.1–3 = fr. 38 and Porphyry,
    Life of Plotinus 24 = 39.
127 See frs 42, 43, 45, 46, 47, 51, 54 and 55.
128 Simplicius, *On Aristotle's* Physics, Corollary on Time = fr. 151B. The phrase 'almost
    everything' in this passage is rather obscure: it could refer to Theophrastus following
    Aristotle on almost all subjects, or in his methodology, or both.
129 Boethius, *On Aristotle's* De interpretatione, *Second edition*, 1 Introduction = fr. 72A.
    Discussion in Sharples 1998: 268.
130 Quintilian, *Oratorical Education* 3.8.62 = fr. 694.
131 Cicero, *On Ends* 1.6 = fr. 50.
132 On the question of divergence see Sharples 1999: 149. Also Fortenbaugh and Har-
    mon 2017.
133 Sharples 1998: 268.
134 On metaphysics see: Sorabji 1998: esp. 204–6. On delivery see Fortenbaugh 2003c.
135 See Porphyry, *On Abstinence from Eating Animals* 2.11.3–15.3 = fr. 584A, discussed
    by Sorabji 1998: esp. 211–20. For a discussion of Theophrastus' contribution to
    modal logic see Mignucci 1998.
136 Baltussen 2016: 8, also 15–17, 34.
137 Baltussen 2016: 4–5.
138 Baltussen 2016: 8.
139 Sharples 1999: 147.
140 Ierodiakonou 2016.
141 Michael Psellus, *Oration* 24.14–18 = fr. 14.
142 See Baltussen 2016: 108–111.
143 See Baltussen 2000: 60–62.
144 Ross 1949: 112.
145 *Metaph.* 8.20 (transl. Ross and Fobes).
146 *HP* 1.3.1. See Hughes 1988, also Fraser 1994.
147 *HP* 1.10.1, 1.11.1, 1.13.1 and 1.14.1.
148 *Lap.* 3 (transl. Caley and Richards).
149 See Anderson 1970: xii.
150 See Trenkner 1958: 147.
151 *CP* 1.5.1, 1.17.8, 1.20.2 and 2.17.1.
152 *CP* 2.14.3–2.16.8.
153 *CP* 5.8.1ff.
154 *CP* 5.8.1 (transl. Einarson and Link).
155 *CP* 1.1.6. Discussed by Fortenbaugh 2003a: 76–7.
156 *Ign.* 1.27 (transl. Coutant).
157 See Hughes 1988: 68 and Trenkner 1958: 147.

158 See Fraser 1994: 171, 177ff.
159 See for example *Lap.* 56 (transl. Caley and Richards).
160 *HP* 5.3.5-6 (transl. Hort).
161 See *HP* 9.8.5–6.
162 See Baltussen 2016: 34, 67.
163 See Baltussen 2000: 120–5, 140–92.
164 Stratton 1917: 16.
165 For a discussion of these standards see Stratton 1917: 56–8.
166 *HP* 5.6.1 (transl. Hort).
167 *HP* 9.17.1.
168 Anderson 1970: xv.
169 Trenkner 1958: 147. Trenkner's judgement seems mainly to be based on Theophrastus' style, which she says (at 148) has no "literary pretentions", but later she appears to contradict this, likening Theophrastus to "a contemporary story-teller" (at 153).
170 Green 1990: 68.
171 See Millett 2007: 17–18.
172 See Millett 2007: 16–17.
173 See Millett 2007: 24.
174 Harpocration, *Lexicon on the Ten Attic Orators*, on bowl-carriers = fr. 653.
175 Suda, on 'more mute than a bowl' = fr.654.
176 See Millett 2007: 24.
177 See Millett 2007: 24.
178 On dress see Athenaeus, *The Sophists at Dinner* 1.38 21A – B = fr. 12.
179 On Theophrastus' speech see frs 5A, 5B, 5D and 7B.
180 See Sollenberger 1992: 3868, also Millett 2007: 20.
181 Lane Fox 1996: 133.
182 Millett 2007: 24.
183 Lane Fox 1996: 156.
184 Lane Fox 1996: 129.
185 See Millett 2007: 56.
186 Lane Fox 1996: 131.
187 Lane Fox 1996: 131–2.
188 Millett 2007: 34. Millett differs from Lane Fox and places the characters as on a "more-or-less uniformly high level". See Millett 2007: 135 n. 121.
189 See Fortenbaugh 2003b: 238.
190 See Lane Fox 1996: 133 and Ussher 1960: 5.

References

Ackrill, J. L. 1981. *Aristotle the Philosopher* (Oxford: Oxford University Press).

Anderson, W. 1970. *Theophrastus: The Character Sketches* (Kent, OH: Kent State University Press).

Baltussen, H. 2000. *Theophrastus against the Presocratics and Plato: Peripatetic Dialectic in the De Sensibus* (Leiden: Brill).

Baltussen, H. 2016. *The Peripatetics: Aristotle's Heirs 322 BCE–200 CE* (London: Routledge).

Boegehold, A. L. 1959. 'The Date of Theophrastus' Characters', *TAPhA* 90: 15–19.

Caley, E. R. and J. C. Richards. 1956. *Theophrastus: On Stones* (Columbus: Ohio State University).

Coutant, V. 1971. *Theophrastus: De Igne* (Assen: Vangorcum).

Diggle, J. 2004. *Theophrastus Characters*. Cambridge Classical Texts and Commentaries 43. (Cambridge: Cambridge University Press).

Einarson, B. and G. K. Link. 1976. *Theophrastus. De Causis Plantarum* Vols. I–III (London: William Heinemann).

Fortenbaugh, W. W. 2003a. 'Theophrastus on Emotion' in TS: 71–90.

Fortenbaugh, W. W. 2003b. 'Theophrastus, the *Characters* and Rhetoric' in TS: 224–243.

Fortenbaugh, W. W. 2003c. 'Theophrastus on Delivery' in TS: 253–271.

Fortenbaugh, W. W. 2005. *Theophrastus of Eresus: Sources for His Life, Writings, Thought and Influence*. Commentary Volume 8: Sources on Rhetoric and Poetics (Texts 666–713) (Leiden: E. J. Brill).

Fortenbaugh, W. W. 2011. *Theophrastus of Eresus*. Commentary Volume 6.1. Sources on Ethics (Leiden: E. J. Brill).

Fortenbaugh, W. W. and R. Harmon. 2017. 'Theophrastus'. In H. Cancik et al. (eds) *Brill's New Pauly*, Brill Reference Online.

Fraser, P.M. 1994. 'The World of Theophrastus'. In S. Hornblower (ed.), *Greek Historiography* (Oxford: Clarendon Press): 167–192.

Furley, D. 1999a. 'Introduction'. In D. Furley (ed.), *Routledge History of Philosophy Vol II From Aristotle to Augustine* (London: Routledge): 1–8.

Furley, D. 1999b. 'Aristotle the Philosopher of Nature'. In D. Furley (ed.), *Routledge History of Philosophy Vol II From Aristotle to Augustine* (London: Routledge): 9–39.

Glucker, J. 1998. 'Theophrastus, the Academy, and the Athenian Philosophical Atmosphere'. In *RUSCH* Vol. VIII: 299–316.

Gotthelf, A. 1988. 'Historiae I: plantarum et animalium'. In *RUSCH* Vol. III: 100–135.

Gottschalk, H. B. 1998. 'Theophrastus and the Peripatos'. In *RUSCH* Vol. VIII: 281–298.

Gottschalk, H. B. 2000. 'Demetrius of Phalerum: A Politician among Philosophers and a Philosopher among Politicians'. In *RUSCH* Vol. IX: 367–380.

Grayeff, F. 1974. *Aristotle and his School* (London: Duckworth).

Green, P. 1990. *Alexander to Actium: The Historical Evolution of the Hellenistic Age* (Berkeley and Los Angeles: University of California Press).

Habicht, C. 1997. *Athens from Alexander to Antony* (Cambridge, MA and London: Harvard University Press).

Hort, A. 1916. *Theophrastus: Enquiry into Plants*. Vols I–II. (London: William Heinemann).

Hughes, J. D. 1988. 'Theophrastus as Ecologist'. In *RUSCH* Vol. III: 67–75.

Ierodiakonou, K. 2016. 'Theophrastus'. *Stanford Encyclopedia of Philosophy*, at https://plato.stanford.edu/entries/theophrastus/ [Accessed January 2017].

Lane Fox, R. 1996. 'Theophrastus' Characters and the Historian', *PCPhS* 42: 127–170.

Long, A. A. 1998. 'Theophrastus and the Stoa'. In *RUSCH* Vol. VIII: 355–383.

Mejer, J. 1998. 'A Life in Fragments. The *Vita Theophrasti*'. In *RUSCH* Vol. VIII: 1–28.

Mignucci, M. 1998. 'Theophrastus' Logic'. In *RUSCH* Vol. VIII: 39–66.

Millett, P. 2007. *Theophrastus and His World*. Proceedings of the Cambridge Philological Society Supplementary Volume 33 (Cambridge: Cambridge University Press).

Navarre, O. 1924. *Caractères de Théophraste: commentaire exégétique et critique* (Paris: Les Belles Lettres).

O'Sullivan, L. 2002. 'The Law of Sophocles and the Beginnings of Permanent Philosophical Schools in Athens', *RhM* 145: 251–262.

O'Sullivan, L. 2009. *The Regime of Demetrius of Phalerum in Athens, 317–307 BCE: A Philosopher in Politics* (Leiden: E. J. Brill).

Ross, W. D. 1949. *Aristotle* (5th ed.) (London: Methuen).

Ross, W. D. and F. H. Fobes 1967. *Theophrastus: Metaphysics* (Hildesheim: George Olms).

Rusten, J. and I. C. Cunningham. 2002. *Theophrastus Characters, Herodas Mimes, Sophron and other Mime Fragments* (Cambridge, MA: Harvard University Press).

Sharples, R. W. 1998. 'Theophrastus as Philosopher and Aristotelian'. In *RUSCH* Vol. VIII: 267–280.

Sharples, R.W. 1999. 'The Peripatetic School'. In D. Furley (ed.), *Routledge History of Philosophy Vol II From Aristotle to Augustine* (London: Routledge): 147–187.

Sollenberger, M. G. 1985. 'Diogenes Laertius 5.36–57: The *Vita Theophrasti*'. In *RUSCH* Vol. II: 1–62.

Sollenberger, M. G. 1992. 'The Lives of the Peripatetics: An Analysis of the Contents and Structure of Diogenes Laertius' "Vitae philosophorum" Book 5', *ANRW* II 36.6, 3793–3879.

Sollenberger, M.G. 2000. 'Diogenes Laertius' Life of Demetrius of Phalerum'. In *RUSCH* Vol. IX: 311–329.

Sorabji, R. 1998. 'Is Theophrastus a Significant Philosopher?'. In *RUSCH* Vol. VIII: 203–221.

Steinmetz, P. 1962. *Theophrast, Charaktere, Das Wort der Antike 7* (Munich: Max Heuber).

Stratton, G. M. 1917. *Theophrastus and the Greek Physiological Psychology before Aristotle* (London: George Allen and Unwin).

Trenkner, S. 1958. *The Greek Novella in the Classical Period* (Cambridge: Cambridge University Press).

Ussher, R. G. 1960. *The Characters of Theophrastus* (London: Macmillan & Co).

Wöhrle, G. 1985. *Theophrasts Methode in seinen botanischen Schriften* (Amsterdam: Grüner).

2 Before and after Theophrastus' *Characters*

The impact of Theophrastus' *Characters* on ancient and modern literature has been remarkably significant and enduring, prompting literary historians to remark that they "cannot think of a smaller book with a greater influence"[1] and that "[o] f all books of Characters, the first remains the best – the 'golden little book' of Theophrastus."[2] This chapter presents a survey of early character descriptions from ancient literature, including poetry, history and philosophical works, all of which focus on generic character types. Theophrastus' approach to character writing was markedly different. Apart from being the first known author to write a dedicated book of character portraits, Theophrastus developed highly realistic and detailed portraits of individuals. Theophrastus also distinguished himself by his compact style and the perceptiveness and humour of his observations. Theophrastus' approach inspired many generations of character writers, especially in England and France in the seventeenth and eighteenth centuries.

Character portraits in Greek, Roman and medieval literature

The earliest surviving example of a character sketch from ancient Greek literature appears in book 2 of Homer's *Iliad*. Thersites, a Greek soldier, is described as unrestrained in his speech and inclined towards slander. His hideous appearance matches his unpleasant character:

> He was the ugliest man of all those that came before Troy – bandy-legged, lame of one foot, with his two shoulders rounded and hunched over his chest. His head ran up to a point, but there was little hair on the top of it. Achilles and Ulysses hated him worst of all, for it was with them that he was most wont to wrangle; now, however, with a shrill squeaky voice he began heaping his abuse on Agamemnon.[3]

The emphasis on unattractive physical attributes as a sign of negative character traits is a concept that persevered in Greek thought well beyond the Homeric period.[4] It is evident many centuries later in the studies of physical attributes conducted by the Peripatetics (discussed in Chapter 3).

A further example of characterisation may be found in book 13 of Homer's *Iliad* amidst scenes of desperate fighting as the Trojans reach the Greek ships.

Idomeneus, the Cretan captain and an outstanding warrior, describes the typical behaviour of a coward in the following terms:

> the coward will change color at every touch and turn; he is full of fears, and keeps shifting his weight first on one knee and then on the other; his heart beats fast as he thinks of death, and one can hear the chattering of his teeth; whereas the brave man will not change color nor be frightened on finding himself in ambush, but is all the time longing to go into action.[5]

Homer's description of the coward is realistic, vivid and concise, and no-one could be better placed to damn cowardly behaviour than the valiant warrior Idomeneus. A portrait of a cowardly type also appears in Theophrastus' *Characters*. Like Homer, Theophrastus focusses on a battle-scene but Theophrastus' *Coward* is a 'real-life' individual rather than a generic type. We observe his conduct as he hides his sword and pretends to look for it (25.4), and we hear his quoted speech, as he lies about having saved a wounded friend from the battle (25.8).

In the seventh century BCE, Semonides of Amorgos employed character portraits in his iambic poetry for a unique purpose.[6] In a darkly satirical entitled *Poem on Women*, Semonides describes ten types of women, each originating from an animal, insect or natural element. There is, for example, a filthy woman crafted from a pig, an evil and cunning woman crafted from a fox, a useless woman crafted from earth, and a moody and changeable woman crafted from the sea:

> Another he made from the sea; she has two characters. One day she smiles and is happy; a stranger who sees her in the house will praise her, and say, 'There is no woman better than this among all mankind, nor more beautiful.' But on another day she is unbearable to look at or come near to; then she raves so that you can't approach her, like a bitch over her pups, and she shows herself ungentle and contrary to enemies and friends alike.[7]

Semonides describes the physical appearance and behaviour of each type of woman with devastating satirical effect. This satire has none of the wit and lightheartedness that we see in Theophrastus' portraits of male character types.

In ancient historical sources, discussions about particular forms of government offered fertile ground for character portraits. Herodotus, for example, paints a damning picture of a monarch in his *Histories*. The words are spoken by a Persian named Otanes, who is arguing in favour of the abolition of the monarchy:

> There is no one better than him at welcoming slander, and there is no one more erratic in his behaviour. I mean, if your admiration for him is moderate, he is offended at your lack of total subservience, and if you are totally subservient, he is angry at you as a flatterer. And now I come to the most important problems with monarchy. A monarch subverts a country's ancestral customs, takes women against their will, and kills men without trial.[8]

Herodotus' description of the monarch's character is given in general, rather than specific, terms. There is no sense of an actual man, in terms of his appearance, speech or manners, as is typical of Theophrastus' *Characters*.

In the *Republic*, Plato devises an innovative way to describe four 'imperfect' forms of political organisation by equating them with four types of character: the Timarchic Man, the Oligarch, the Democrat, and the Tyrant.[9] The Timarchic Man is the sort who is ambitious, arrogant and athletic, a lover of honour but lacking in properly trained reason and imagination.[10] The Oligarch is entirely preoccupied with making money, which makes him avaricious, squalid and a hoarder.[11] The Democrat lacks decency and restraint. He seeks freedom, happiness and pleasure in all things.[12] The Tyrant is the epitome of a criminal. He is driven by lust, behaves violently, and lacks true friends and supporters.[13] Theophrastus continues this tradition of 'political' character writing with a detailed character portrait of the *Oligarchic Man*, as well as other types who display inappropriate behaviour in political contexts (for example, the *Tactless Man* and the *Arrogant Man*).

Aristotle uses descriptions of character types to illustrate particular ethical points. In his discussion of virtues and vices in the *Nicomachean Ethics* (discussed in Chapter 4), Aristotle examines different forms of conduct, labelling some forms excessive, others deficient and some as appropriately balanced between the two extremes.[14] There is, for example, the cowardly man who fears too much,[15] the rash man who fears too little[16] and the courageous man who shows the right response according to the circumstances.[17] Aristotle sets out thirteen trios of virtues and vices of characters, and he describes most of these virtues and vices in detail.[18] The critical point to note is that Aristotle describes his ethical types in abstract terms and without any humour. His ethical characters are philosophical and abstract generalisations.[19] As Diggle puts it, they are "moral paradigms, not flesh and blood".[20] Aristotle describes the sort of behaviour one would expect from a particular type, investigating the causes of that behaviour and explaining emotions.[21] In contrast, Theophrastus' character types are very much 'flesh and blood' individuals and Theophrastus gives no analysis of behaviour or motives.[22]

Apart from Aristotle's ethical works, there are also character portraits in Aristotle's *Rhetoric*, including three distinct portraits of young, middle-aged and old men.[23] Again, Aristotle describes these types in abstract terms. Old men are described as follows:

> [O]wing to their having lived many years and having been more often deceived by others or made more mistakes themselves, and since most human things turn out badly, they are positive about nothing, and in everything they show an excessive lack of energy. They always "think," but "know" nothing; and in their hesitation they always add "perhaps," or "maybe"; all their statements are of this kind, never unqualified.[24]

Aristotle's use of quoted speech anticipates Theophrastus' method. The topics that Aristotle relies on to indicate character, namely manner of speech, and attitude to life, people, money and property, are also evident in Theophrastus' characterisation of types.

At some point in the late fourth century, Theophrastus' character portraits were committed to writing. In his work, Theophrastus focusses on one individual and character trait at a time, placing him in an everyday setting; describing his appearance, dress and typical manners; and having him 'act out' typical modes of speech and conduct. The impression is that Theophrastus' portraits are of 'real' individuals, not the abstract cowards, monarchs, oligarchs, or old men who were the predecessors of the *Characters*. Theophrastus' genius lies in his careful method and simple design.[25] He starts by meticulously gathering examples of what a particular type of man habitually does or says. He then selects examples that are insightful, interesting and amusing, presenting these examples using simple language and carefully layering the examples in order to build humour and impact. The result is a skilfully crafted, compact and precise portrait of an individual man who also represents a type.[26] Theophrastus' *Tactless Man* provides a clear example:

> The Tactless Man is the kind who comes for a discussion when you are busy. He serenades his girlfriend when she is feverish. He approaches a man who has just forfeited a security deposit and asks him to stand bail. He arrives to give evidence after a case is closed. As a guest at a wedding he delivers a tirade against the female sex. When you have just returned home after a long journey he invites you to go for a walk. He is liable to bring along a higher bidder when you have already completed a sale. When the audience has taken the point he gets up to explain it all over again.

The realism and humour of Theophrastus' character descriptions is unique in Greek literature. While Aristotle analyses the attributes and motives of the boastful man in serious terms, for example, Theophrastus presents the *Boastful Man*'s actual words as reported speech (23.2–9). In this way, the *Boastful Man* appears to reveal himself to the audience through his own conduct, speech and manners. We observe the *Boastful Man* just as we would observe a character on stage. Theophrastus remains outside of the narrative but his sharp insight, combined with the masterful arrangement of his material and his flair for comic exaggeration, indicate comic method combined with serious ethical purpose.

After the appearance of Theophrastus' *Characters* in the late fourth century, we can trace the influence of the work through subsequent Peripatetic authors into Roman literature.[27] The Peripatetic Satyrus, for example, who lived in the third to second centuries BCE, wrote a work entitled *Concerning Character*, from which a fragmentary description of a profligate type remains.[28] Lyco of Troas (c. 300–225 BCE), who was the fourth and longest-serving head of the Peripatos,[29] also wrote character portraits. His description of a drunkard reeling from a party the night before is both vivid and memorable:[30]

> Satiated with too much food and drink from a former day, at noon he is with difficulty awakened drunk, first with eyes wet with wine, blinded with

moisture, heavy, unable to look at the light steadily; exhausted because his veins are filled with wine rather than blood, he cannot raise himself.[31]

Although Lyco clearly continued the tradition of Theophrastean character writing[32] his sketch differs from Theophrastus' character portraits in significant ways. Lyco's narrative follows the drunkard over the course of a single day[33] rather than skipping between scenes and settings as Theophrastus does. The style is more embellished than that of Theophrastus,[34] and the subject is wider, describing the behaviour of the drunkard as well as other guests.

Lyco was succeeded by Aristo of Keos,[35] who wrote a work entitled *On Relief from Arrogance*. This work is partially preserved in a later source[36] and it contains four character portraits namely, the Inconsiderate Man, the Self-Willed Man, the Know-it-all and the Dissembler.[37] At first glance, there are some obvious similarities between these types and Theophrastus' *Characters*, particularly the emphasis on negative character traits, common subjects and stylistic similarities,[38] but there are crucial differences too. Unlike Theophrastus' work, a detailed commentary has been added to Aristo's descriptions (most likely by Philodemus, the author of the overall work). The commentary is laboured and obvious.[39] It demonstrates that when character portraits are artfully constructed, as in Theophrastus' collection, commentary is superfluous.

Throughout Roman times, characterisation was an important part of training in the rhetorical arts.[40] In a work by the rhetorician Rutilius Lupus entitled *On Figures of Thought and Style*,[41] Rutilius states that just as a painter uses colours to represent figures, an orator uses characterisation to delineate the virtues and vices of the individual he wishes to describe and he quotes Lyco's drunkard as an example of this technique.[42] Characterising an individual as virtuous or unvirtuous could be important in the context of courtroom speeches, to exonerate or discredit a witness or plaintiff. It could also be important in ceremonial discourse, for the purposes of praising or censuring a public figure, and in deliberative discourse, to persuade for or against a particular course of action. For this reason, descriptions of various character types, such as Theophrastus', were highly valued by orators. In fact, the survival of the text of the *Characters* is primarily due to rhetoricians such as Hermogenes of Tarsus who, in the second century CE, referred to Theophrastus' character portraits and incorporated them into their rhetorical handbooks.[43]

The unknown author of the rhetorical handbook known as the *Rhetorica ad Herennium* from the first century BCE draws a distinction between descriptions of a person's physical appearance and descriptions of character, known as *notatio*:

Notatio is the description of the nature of someone by definite signs, certain marks, as it were, bestowed upon that disposition. Suppose you wished to describe someone who is not rich but is ostentatious with his money. You might say, 'That man, judges, who thinks it is wonderful to be thought rich, just look at him as he gazes at us. . . . When indeed he has smoothed his beard with his left hand he thinks that his appearance far outshines that of anyone else because of the gleam of his gems and the lustre of his gold.' [44]

The text goes on to describe how the ostentatious type invites people to dinner and then tricks them into thinking that he owns a more expensive house than he actually does. This description reads like an extended character sketch written in Theophrastean style[45] and there are similarities with Theophrastus' sketch of the *Boastful Man* (23) and the *Man of Petty Ambition* (21).[46]

Cicero, one of the foremost Roman orators, does not refer explicitly to Theophrastus' *Characters* but, when he describes reading Theophrastus' writing as his 'private pleasure',[47] it is tempting to think he might have been referring to the *Characters*. He was certainly aware of Theophrastus and makes reference to his works many times in his own treatises *On the Orator*,[48] *On Invention*[49] and *Orator*.[50] Cicero also mentions him favourably alongside Aristotle and Plato.[51] On the subject of character, Cicero recognises that character drawing is an essential element of an orator's art, especially in defining and analysing the particular qualities of one's subject.[52] Cicero's term for character delineation is *descriptio*. As an example of *descriptio*, Cicero says that one might describe a miser, or a flatterer or some other type, along with a description of his character and ways of life.[53] Portraits of the miserly type (10) and the flatterer (2) appear in Theophrastus' *Characters*.

The Roman rhetorician known as Quintilian was also familiar with Theophrastus and he refers to Theophrastus' work many times in his rhetorical handbook entitled *Oratorical Education*.[54] Quintilian states that character drawing is essential for orators.[55] In particular, he advises orators to practise characterisation by impersonating "sons, parents, rich men, old men, the bad-tempered, the easygoing, misers, the superstitious, cowards or mockers; comic actors hardly have more roles to sustain in their performance than these men do in their speeches."[56] This advice is particularly insightful in highlighting the closeness between the impersonation of character by orators and the portrayal of character by comic actors, and because miserly men, superstitious men, cowards and 'mockers' all feature in Theophrastus' *Characters* (see types 10, 16, 25 and 1). Quintilian also reports that Theophrastus recommended that orators read poetry in order to learn how to characterise people and emotions properly.[57]

In Roman literature of the first century BCE onwards, the character portrait became a favourite literary device, especially for the satirists. In his *Satires*, Horace gives an amusing account of an unfortunate encounter with an Irritating Man.[58] This character type is reminiscent of some of Theophrastus' types, especially the *Talker*, and just as in Theophrastus' portraits, there is a pronounced use of quoted speech. Horace's Irritating Man says: "You're dreadfully anxious to be off. . . . I have long seen that; but it's no use, I'll stick to you; I'll stay with you to your journey's end."[59] Unlike Theophrastus' character portraits, however, Horace's satirical portrait provides an insight into the narrator's private thoughts as he tries to escape. Arguably, Horace's character portrait focusses more on the narrator's reaction to the Irritating Man than the character type himself.

The Roman poet Martial offers an amusing character portrait of the 'pretty fellow' or *bellus homo*.[60] The description is so compact that it can be quoted in its entirety:

> A pretty fellow curls his hair and arranges it carefully, always smells of balsam or cinnamon, hums tunes from the Nile and from Gades, moves his plucked arms in time with changing measures, lounges all day among ladies' chairs and is ever a-murmuring into some ear, reads billets sent from this quarter and that, and writes them, shrinks from the cloak on a neighbor's elbow, knows who's in love with whom, scurries from dinner party to dinner party, has Hirpinus' ancient pedigree by heart.[61]

Martial displays the same closeness of observation and delight in gesture and manner that is evident in Theophrastus' character portraits, and his description of the 'pretty fellow' shrinking from making contact with his neighbour's cloak is delightfully Theophrastean in its vividness.

Juvenal, a Roman satirist and poet, incorporates a character portrait into his fourteenth satire in which he bemoans the poor example that parents often set for their children. To illustrate this, Juvenal gives a character portrait of a Miser:[62]

> He punishes his slaves' bellies with unfair rations and goes hungry himself. The fact is that he can't even bear to eat up all the mouldy hunks of his blue-green bread. He habitually keeps yesterday's mincemeat in the middle of September and, yes, in summer he puts aside his beans till the next dinnertime, sealed up with a bit of mackerel or half a rotting sprat, and he puts away the shreds of chopped leek only after they've been counted. Any beggar from a bridge who's invited to this meal would refuse.[63]

As with Theophrastus' character portraits, the description is memorable for its vivid realism and the precise manner in which the examples of behaviour illustrate the particular character trait. Juvenal also wrote character portraits of female types in his infamous sixth satire, such as the shameless Eppia infatuated with her beloved gladiator,[64] the sex-crazed Messalina,[65] the tiresomely learned wife with her perfect knowledge of Greek,[66] and the woman obsessed with makeup and dress.[67]

In the first century CE, the Stoic philosopher Seneca adapted the character portrait for his own philosophical purposes. Seneca's portrait of the Happy Man reverses many of the undesirable character traits identified by Theophrastus (such as penuriousness, arrogance and cowardice) in order to set out a rare example of a positive character type.[68] As we saw in Aristotle's philosophical works, Seneca develops a moral paradigm and the tone of his work, rather than being humorous and realistic, is serious and exalted.

In roughly the same period, Lucian of Samosata, an ancient Greek rhetorician and satirist writing in Syria, appears to have been familiar with the *Characters*. His work contains proverbs and phrases that appear in the *Characters*[69] and a number of passages similar to the *Characters*.[70] Portions of Theophrastus' descriptions of the *Coward* and the *Oligarchic Man* are also preserved in papyri dating from the third century CE.[71] In the fourth century CE, the text of Theophrastus' *Characters* was incorporated into the rhetorical treatise written by Aphthonius of Antioch.[72]

In Arabic sources, there is no mention of the *Characters* although other Theophrastean works are discussed, particularly his works on *Metaphysics* and *Meteorology*.[73] There are also references to Theophrastus' life in Arabic sources,[74] the oldest of which is the *Fihrist* of Ibn al-Nadim, completed in 987 AD.[75] According to Daiber, "Theophrastus was known to the Arabs as a man of many accomplishments," and especially as "an authority in metaphysics, psychology, meteorology, botany, physics, and logic".[76] Byzantine scholars also cite Theophrastus' works with approval. For example, Theophrastus' scientific treatises are widely referred to by the Patriarch Photius in the ninth century.[77] But it is not until the twelfth century that Theophrastus' *Characters* are again mentioned, by the Byzantine poet and grammarian Ioannes Tzetzes[78] and Eustathius, the archbishop of Thessaloniki.[79]

In the medieval period, it seems that both Theophrastus and the *Characters* largely disappeared from view.[80] This is despite a strong interest in character in literature and the development of exemplary characters who personified virtues (such as Raison in *Roman de La Rose*), and 'typical' characters such as kings, knights and maidens.[81] Geoffrey Chaucer's characters in the *Canterbury Tales* stand out in this period for their realism and for Chaucer's use of wit and irony.[82] Furthermore, Chaucer appears to have been familiar with Theophrastus' writings as *The Wife of Bath's Prologue* is closely modelled upon (and quotes directly from) Theophrastus' sketch of the typical wife in his treatise *On Marriage* (discussed in Chapter 5).[83]

Character writers of the modern era

Theophrastus' *Characters* appeared on the modern literary landscape when the first edition of the work was published at Nuremberg in 1527, with a translation in Latin, and a dedication to the famous portrait painter Albrecht Dürer.[84] A further nine editions of the *Characters* were published in the sixteenth century, culminating in the widely acclaimed edition by Isaac Casaubon in 1592.[85] For the first time, Theophrastus' character portraits were available to an educated public[86] and Casaubon's textual emendations and detailed commentary made sense of the *Characters* for a wider audience.[87]

In the seventeenth century, Theophrastus' collection of character portraits gained great popularity and influence among European writers, particularly in England and France. Theophrastus' work served as an example of the art of character writing and its critical features, including precision, humour and compactness.[88] Although the character portraits composed by later authors very often differ from Theophrastus', there is a "conscious artistic succession",[89] which becomes apparent when we compare Theophrastus' character portraits with some of his imitators.

In 1608, the English satirist Joseph Hall wrote his *Characters of Virtues and Vices*.[90] Hall adapted the Theophrastean character for the purposes of Christian moralising, and his collection of character types includes a handful of virtuous types, such as the Humble Man and the True Friend, and a veritable panorama of degraded ones, including the Hypocrite, the Busybody, the Vainglorious and the Slothful. It is useful to compare Theophrastus' *Toady* with Hall's portrait of the Flatterer, in order to see how each author deals with essentially the same material. Theophrastus says:

> The Toady is the sort of man who says to a person walking with him 'Are you aware of the admiring looks you are getting? This doesn't happen to anyone else in the city except you' . . . . And he asks him if he is chilly and wants to put something on, and before the words are out of his mouth he wraps him up.
>
> (2.2,10)

Hall's version is as follows:

> Let him say it is hot, he wipes his forehead and unbraceth himself; if cold, he shivers and calls for a warmer garment. When he walks with his friend he swears to him that no man else is looked at, no man talked of, and that whomsoever he vouchsafes to look on and nod to is graced enough.[91]

In 1614, a book of character portraits written by Sir Thomas Overbury was published posthumously.[92] Overbury was masterful at painting witty character portraits of types drawn from different professions and social classes, including the Fair and Happy Milk Maid, the Fine Gentleman, the Pirate, and the French Cook. There is a noticeable difference in style and method, as Overbury's portraits are descriptive, whereas Theophrastus' are illustrative. We can observe this in their respective portraits of the *Dissembler*. Theophrastus says as follows:

> He pretends not to have heard, claims not to have seen, and says that he does not remember agreeing. Sometimes he says that he will think about it, at other times that he has no idea, or that he is surprised, or that he once had the same thought himself. In general he is a great one for using expressions like 'I don't believe it', 'I can't imagine it', 'I am amazed'.
>
> (1.5–6)

Overbury says the following:

> [A Dissembler i]s an essence needing a double definition, for he is not that (sic) he appears. Unto the eye he is pleasing, unto the ear he is harsh, but unto the understanding intricate and full of windings; he is the *prima materia*, and his intents give him form; he dyeth his means and his meaning into two colours; he baits craft with humility, and his countenance is the picture of the present disposition.[93]

In John Earle's *Microcosmography*, published in 1628,[94] there are many delightful and philosophical character portraits that reflect Theophrastean simplicity, such as his sketch of A Meddling Man, A Flatterer, and A Sordid Rich Man. Earle has a good grip on Theophrastus' humour and eye for detail. Earle's sketch of A Plain Country Fellow is closely modelled upon Theophrastus' *Country Bumpkin*. Theophrastus' description is as follows:

> The Country Bumpkin is the sort of man who drinks a bowl of gruel before going to the Assembly and claims that garlic smells as sweet as perfume, wears shoes too large for his feet and talks at the top of his voice. . . . In the street the only sight in which he takes any <pleasure> or interest is an ox or a donkey or a goat, at which he will stop and stare. He is apt to raid the larder and drink his wine neat. . . . He gives the plough-animals <their fodder> while eating his breakfast.

(4.2–9)

Earle's portrait of the same type is as follows:

> [H]is conversation is among beasts, and his talons none of the shortest, only he eats not grass, because he loves not salads. . . . He expostulates with his oxen very understandingly, and speaks gee, and ree, better than English. His mind is not much distracted with objects, but if a good fat cow come in his way, he stands dumb and astonished, and though his haste be never so great, will fix here half an hour's contemplation.[95]

The poet and satirist Samuel Butler wrote one hundred and twenty character portraits.[96] These were published in 1759 in a collection known simply as the *Characters*, alongside some of his other writings.[97] Butler is a master of simile and metaphor and he shows a great deal of interest in the psychology of his character types, describing their intentions, motivations and desires. Theophrastus simply reports the speech and conduct of his characters in straightforward terms without psychological analysis. Despite these differences, there are still echoes of Theophrastus in Butler's choice of subjects, as we can see in their treatment of talkative types. Theophrastus' *Talker* is described as follows:

> On a jury he prevents others from reaching a verdict, at the theatre from watching the play, at dinner from getting on with their meal. He says 'It's hard for me to keep quiet'; that he has a well-oiled tongue; and that, even if he might appear to twitter more than a swallow, he will still not shut up. He does not even mind being the butt of his children's jokes. . . . 'Talk to us, daddy,' they say, 'and send us to sleep.'

(7.8–10)

We can compare this with Butler's portrait of the Prater:

> He is like an earwig; when he gets within a man's ear he is not easily to be got out again. He will stretch a story as unmercifully as he does the ears of those he tells it to, and draw it out in length like a breast of mutton at the Hercules

pillars, or a piece of cloth set on the tenters, till it is quite spoiled and good for nothing.[98]

In 1688, the French moralist Jean de La Bruyère published his own book of characters entitled *Les Caractères, ou les Moeurs de ce Siècle*. The first edition contained a translation of Theophrastus' *Characters* from Greek, followed by two hundred pages of essays by La Bruyère.[99] The work was an overnight success in France. Two further editions appeared that year, with nine editions published in total.[100] La Bruyère was careful to explain his methodology saying: "I seek only to work within that branch of knowledge which describes behaviour, studies men and develops their character."[101] Despite this, readers related the work to descriptions of the court of France and the French nation,[102] and it became a popular sport to try to identify the individuals being targeted by La Bruyère.[103] Today, La Bruyère's *Characters* are considered to be a masterpiece of French literature and it is widely recognised that he adopted Theophrastus' technique of presenting character types with a view to making moral criticisms.

The tradition of character writing reached a high point in the seventeenth century and was continued in later centuries by many writers including Alexander Pope, W.M. Thackeray in his *Great City Snobs* and Charles Dickens. George Eliot, in her novel *Impressions of Theophrastus Such* published in 1879, offered a critique of her own society and times through the eyes of Theophrastus.[104] The popularity of character writing after Theophrastus demonstrates that he touched upon a subject of great interest and relevance. The character portrait proved to be highly adaptable and able to be moulded to a variety of purposes, including moralising, social criticism, satire and characterisation in the novel.[105] Although authors have developed character types that are illustrative of their own societies and times, Theophrastus' character portraits have maintained their primacy as unparalleled examples of simplicity, precision, brevity and wit.

Notes

1 Smeed 1985: 5.
2 Ussher 1960: 31.
3 Homer, *Iliad* 2.216–222, transl. Butler (Loeb).
4 Vogt 2006: 264.
5 Homer, *Iliad* 13.278–286, transl. Butler (Loeb).
6 Lloyd-Jones 1975: 23.
7 Semonides, *Poem on Women*, transl. Lloyd-Jones: 43.
8 Herodotus, *Histories* 3.80.5, transl. Waterfield and Dewald.
9 Pappas 2013: 266ff.
10 Pl. *R.* 547D–548E.
11 Pl. *R.* 551A–B.
12 Pl. *R.* 561A–E.
13 Pl. *R.* 566A–D.
14 *EN* 2.8.1–2 (1108b11–18).
15 *EN* 3.7.10–12 (1115b34–1116a4).
16 *EN* 3.7.7–9. (1115b24–34).

17 *EN* 3.7.13 (1116a10–16).
18 For a brief account of the virtues and vices see *EN* 2.7.1–2.7.16 (1107b1–1108b10). More detailed descriptions appear at *EN* 3.6.1–5.11.10 (1115a6–1138b16). There is a different list of vices in *EE* 2.3.4 (1220b38–1221a12).
19 Baltussen 2016: 88; Rusten and Cunningham 2002: 20.
20 Diggle 2004: 7. Also see Ussher 1960: 11.
21 Boyce 1967: 13.
22 Rusten and Cunningham 2002: 20.
23 *Rh.* 2.12.1–2.14.4 (1389a–1390b).
24 *Rh.* 2.13.1–3 (1389b, transl. Freese).
25 Boyce 1967: 9–10.
26 Boyce 1967: 177.
27 See Boyce 1967: 11–36.
28 Diggle 2004: 11.
29 Baltussen 2016: 10.
30 Rutilius Lupus, *De figuris* 2.7 = Text 12 in Fortenbaugh and White 2004: 48–52. Also see Boyce 1967: 22–3, Diggle 2004: 9. It has been suggested that the sketch came from a lost work *On Drunkenness*: see Fortenbaugh 2011: 139.
31 This translation is from Boyce 1967: 22.
32 Fortenbaugh 2011: 139.
33 See Diggle 2004: 9. Fortenbaugh argues that considerable care has been taken to select and arrange the scenes: Fortenbaugh 2004: 434–5.
34 Diggle's judgement is harsh: "colours garish, rhetoric over-dressed, cleverness unremitting" (Diggle 2004: 9).
35 See Baltussen 2016: 10–11.
36 Philodemus, *On Vices*, Book 10. See text and translation in Rusten and Cunningham 2002: 160–75.
37 For commentary see Vogt 2006: 271–8.
38 Fortenbaugh observes that the "ethical orientation of Aristo's work encourages treating Theophrastus' *Characters* as similarly oriented": Fortenbaugh 2011: 140. For analysis of stylistic similarities see Diggle 2004: 10.
39 Millett 2007 at 12 refers to the commentary as "ponderous" but Rusten and Cunningham 2002: 182 more accurately label it as "tedious and contorted".
40 On the character of the speaker see Corbett and Connors 1999: 19. On character in invective see Arena 2007.
41 Rutilius Lupus, *De figuris*, 2.7 = Text 12 in Fortenbaugh and White 2004: 48–52.
42 See Fortenbaugh 2004: 434.
43 Diggle 2004: 13 n. 42.
44 Text and translation in Boyce 1967: 24–5.
45 See Boyce 1967: 26–7.
46 See Diggle 2004: 12, n. 37.
47 Plutarch, *Cicero* 24.5–6 = fr. 53.
48 See frs. 667–8, 701 and 713.
49 See fr. 674.
50 See frs. 684, 697, 699, 700, 702 and 704.
51 For examples of Cicero's positive comments about Theophrastus see frs. 46, 50, 51, 52A, 52B, 56 and 669.
52 Cic. *Top.* 83.
53 Cic. *Top.* 83.
54 See frs. 7B, 670, 671, 680, 694 and 707.
55 Quint. *Inst.* 3.8.50.
56 Quint. *Inst.* 3.8.51 transl. Russell (Loeb).
57 Quint. *Inst.* 10.1.27 = fr. 707.

58 Hor. *Sat.* 1.9.
59 Hor. *Sat.* 1.9.13–15. transl. by Fairclough (Loeb).
60 Mart. *Ep.* 3.63.
61 Mart. *Ep.* 3.63 transl. Shackleton Bailey (Loeb).
62 Juv. *Sat.* 14.109–134.
63 Juv. *Sat.* 14.126–134 transl. Morton Braund (Loeb)
64 Juv. *Sat.* 6.82–113.
65 Juv. *Sat.* 6.114–135.
66 Juv. *Sat.* 6.184–199.
67 Juv. *Sat.* 6.457–473; for discussion see Boyce 1967: 92.
68 Sen. *Ep.* 45.9–10.
69 Macleod 1974: 76.
70 Baldwin 1977: 174–5.
71 Diggle 2004: 25–6.
72 Diggle 2004: 13, n. 42.
73 See Daiber 1985 and Gutas 1985.
74 See for example frs. 3A, 3B and 41.
75 For discussion see Gutas 1985.
76 Daiber 1985: 103.
77 Photius quotes at length from Theophrastus' books *On Paralysis* (see fr. 346); *On Fainting* (fr. 345), *On Creatures that Appear in Swarms* (fr. 359A), *On Creatures Said to be Grudging* (fr. 362A); and *On Types of Honey* (fr. 435).
78 Tzetzes, *Histories* 9.934 = fr. 436 no. 4c.
79 Eustathius, *Commentaries on the* Iliad 13.276 = fr. 436.4c; for discussion see Diggle 2004: 6, 19, 26.
80 Schmitt 1971.
81 Ginsberg 1983: 78.
82 Chaucer's method is discussed by Boyce 1967: 33–6.
83 Compare Chaucer, *The Wife of Bath's Prologue* 669–85 with Theophrastus, *On Marriage* quoted in Jerome, *Against Jovinian* 1.47–8 = fr. 486. This directly contradicts Ussher's claim that "Chaucer knew naught of Theophrastus": Ussher 1960: 30. See also Ginsberg 1983: 134.
84 In 1430, Lapo da Castiglionchio produced a Latin translation of Theophrastus' *Characters* but this only appeared in a later edition published in Basel by A. Cratander in 1531. The *editio princeps* is therefore considered to be the edition by Pirckheimer published at Nuremberg in 1527. On Dürer: see Diggle 2004: 52.
85 On Casaubon's various editions see Diggle 2004: 53.
86 Anderson 1970: xxii.
87 Rusten and Cunningham 2002: 34.
88 See Anderson 1970: xxii. Jebb-Sandys: 22–32.
89 Boyce 1967: 53.
90 Morley 1891: 108.
91 J. Hall, 'Of the Flatterer' from *Characters of Virtues and Vices*, as reprinted in Morley 1891: 139–40.
92 See Anderson 1970: xxiii. Rusten and Cunningham 2002: 37–8.
93 Sir T. Overbury, 'A Dissembler' from *Characters; or Witty Descriptions of the Properties of Sundry Persons*, as reprinted in Morley 1891: 31.
94 Morley 1891: 154.
95 J. Earle, 'A Plain Country Fellow' from *Microcosmography; or A Piece of the World Characterized*, as reprinted in Morley 1891: 182.
96 Morley 1891: 316.
97 Morley 1891: 316.
98 S. Butler, 'A Prater' from *Characters*, as reprinted in Morley 1891: 348.

99   Knox 1973: 22.
100 See Knox 1973: 11.
101 Knox 1973: 25.
102 See discussion in Millett 2007: 12–13. Also Van Laun 1929: ii.
103 Ussher 1960: 29.
104 For a more detailed history of character writing see Smeed 1985 and Greenough 1947.
105 See Ussher 1960: 26, 31.

References

Anderson, W. 1970. *Theophrastus: The Character Sketches* (Kent, OH: Kent State University Press).

Arena, V. 2007. 'Roman Oratorical Invective'. In W. Dominik and J. Hall (eds). *A Companion to Roman Rhetoric* (Malden, MA: Blackwell): 149–160.

Baldwin, B. 1977. 'Lucian and Theophrastus', *Mnemosyne* 30.2: 174–176.

Baltussen, H. 2016. *The Peripatetics: Aristotle's Heirs 322 BCE–200 CE* (London: Routledge).

Boyce, B. 1967. *The Theophrastan Character in England to 1642* (London: Frank Cass & Co.).

Corbett, E. and R. Connors. 1999. *Classical Rhetoric for the Modern Student 4th ed.* (New York, Oxford: Oxford University Press).

Daiber, H. 1985. 'A Survey of Theophrastean Texts and Ideas in Arabic: Some New Material'. In *RUSCH* Vol. II: 103–114.

Diggle, J. 2004. *Theophrastus Characters*. Cambridge Classical Texts and Commentaries 43. (Cambridge: Cambridge University Press).

Fortenbaugh, W. W. 2004. 'Lyco φραστικός: Comments on Ten Texts'. In Fortenbaugh and White: 411–441.

Fortenbaugh, W. W. 2011. *Theophrastus of Eresus*. Commentary Volume 6.1. Sources on Ethics (Leiden: E. J. Brill).

Fortenbaugh, W. W. and S. White (eds). 2004. *Lyco of Troas and Hieronymus of Rhodes: Text, Translation and Discussion RUSCH Vol. XII* (New Brunswick and London: Routledge).

Ginsberg, W. 1983. *The Cast of Character: The Representation of Personality in Ancient and Medieval Literature* (Toronto: University of Toronto Press).

Gordon, G. S. 1912. *English Literature and the Classics* (New York: Russell and Russell).

Greenough, C. N. 1947. *A Bibliography of the Theophrastan Character in English with Several Portrait Characters* (Harvard: Harvard University Press).

Gutas, D. 1985. 'The Life, Works, and Sayings of Theophrastus in the Arabic Tradition'. In *RUSCH* Vol. II: 63–102.

Knox, E. C. 1973. *Jean de la Bruyère* (New York: Twayne Publishers).

Lloyd-Jones, H. 1975. *Females of the Species: Semonides on Women* (London: Duckworth).

Macleod, M. D. 1974. 'Lucian's Knowledge of Theophrastus', *Mnemosyne* 27.1: 75–76.

Millett, P. 2007. *Theophrastus and His World*. Proceedings of the Cambridge Philological Society Supplementary Volume 33 (Cambridge: Cambridge University Press).

Morley, H. (ed.) 1891. *Character Writings of the Seventeenth Century* (London: George Routledge and Sons).

Pappas, N. 2013. *The Routledge Guidebook to Plato's Republic* (London and New York: Routledge).

Rusten, J. and I. C. Cunningham. 2002. *Theophrastus Characters, Herodas Mimes, Sophron and Other Mime Fragments* (Cambridge, MA: Harvard University Press).

Schmitt, C. B. 1971. 'Theophrastus in the Middle Ages', *Viator* 2: 251–270.

Smeed, J. W. 1985. *The Theophrastan 'Character': The History of a Literary Genre* (Oxford: Clarendon Press).

Ussher, R. G. 1960. *The Characters of Theophrastus* (London: Macmillan & Co).

Van Laun, H. 1929. *The Characters of Jean de la Bruyère* (New York: Brentano's).

Vogt, S. 2006. 'Characters in Aristo'. In W. W. Fortenbaugh and S. White (eds). *Aristo of Ceos: Text, Translation and Discussion RUSCH* Vol. XIII (New Brunswick: Transaction): 261–278.

Waterfield, R. and C. Dewald. 1998. Herodotus. *The Histories* (Oxford: Oxford University Press).

3   The *Characters* as a comedy of manners

Theophrastus' character portraits are written with a deliberate and thoughtful use of humour that gives pleasure to the reader[1] and adds colour and vibrancy to the underlying ethical purpose of the work. This use of humour reflects Theophrastus' wider interest in the subject of comedy and, specifically, his definition of comedy as a 'concealed rebuke for error'. As head of the Peripatos, Theophrastus' interest in comedy and ethics also had an impact on developments that were taking place in the comic theatre of Athens. In particular, Theophrastus' teachings influenced Menander, who studied under Theophrastus and later proved to be one of the foremost comic playwrights of the fourth century BCE. Traces of Theophrastus' philosophical views in Menander's comedies indicate a direct Peripatetic influence on Athenian comic drama.

Theophrastus on comedy

Theophrastus had a keen interest in the subject of comedy. He wrote two works directly on the subject of comedy, entitled *On the Ludicrous*[2] and *On Comedy*,[3] as well as more general works, such as *On the Art of Poetry*[4] and *On Expression*.[5] We have already noted Theophrastus' tendency to include amusing anecdotes even in his serious scientific treatises (Chapter 1). Anecdotes in the ancient sources also attest to his penchant for humour and his reputation for quick wit and clever repartee. When Theophrastus encountered a chatterbox, for example, he is reported to have said: "Tomorrow, where will it be possible not to see you?"[6] Theophrastus is also reported to have made fun of a man with a snub nose, saying "I am amazed at your eyes, for they do not sing, though your nose gives them the pitch."[7]

Although Theophrastus' works on comedy have unfortunately been lost, fragments of his views on comedy survive in various sources. Theophrastus is mentioned in a discussion about four kinds of dramatic poetry: comedy, tragedy, satyric drama and mime.[8] In defining the differences between tragedy and comedy, Theophrastus is reported to have said that "[t]ragedy is a crisis of heroic fortune" while "[c]omedy is an account of private and civic fortune without danger to life."[9] If this passage is truly representative of Theophrastus' views,[10] then it indicates a correspondence between Theophrastus' view of comedy and the subject of the *Characters*, which focusses on ordinary people engaged in private and everyday matters.

In his work *On Comedy*, Theophrastus is said to have related a story about the people of Tiryns, who enjoyed laughter so much that they were prevented from engaging in serious matters.[11] Even after consulting the Delphic oracle for advice, they were unable to cure their habit of laughter.[12] This story reminds us of Theophrastus' *Characters* because here too the characters suffer from behavioural traits that are humorous and seemingly permanent,[13] such as obtuseness, arrogance and repulsiveness. Even when the character types are aware of their deficiencies, they seem to be either unable or unwilling to address them. The *Offensive Man*, for example, takes pride in his congenital ailments and does not attend to them (19.2) and the *Talker* admits that it is hard for him to keep quiet but still does not stop (7.9).

Theophrastus and Aristotle are also reported to have held the view that comedy should be harmless.[14] In the *Poetics*, Aristotle focusses on the pleasure of comedy as an imitative artform and he says that comedy is an imitation of types of men who exhibit "any fault or mark of shame which involves no pain or destruction".[15] In referring to 'faulty' or 'shameful' attributes, Aristotle is referring to physical features as well as moral ones. The important point is that laughing at these sorts of deficiencies should not cause pain to the subject in question.[16]

Theophrastus' *Characters* illustrate in a practical way Aristotle's requirement that an error or deformity should be harmless in order for it to have comic impact. Some of Theophrastus' *Characters* are physically deformed, such as the *Offensive Man*, with his flaky skin and black nails (19.2), while others are morally defective, such as the *Coward* who mistakes every headland for a looming pirate ship (25.2). In both cases, the deficiencies are harmless, which keeps the subject within the realm of the comic and outside the 'unfunny' realms of the truly grotesque, deplorable or abhorrent. In other words, Theophrastus maintains a lightness of touch in his humour so as to keep it from becoming unduly harsh or unkind. This is in keeping with Theophrastus' view that "the subjects of jokes ought to be the sort at which the listener is delighted and the speaker is not ashamed."[17]

Theophrastus' definition of comedy

The most important insight into Theophrastus' theory of comedy is his definition of a comic jest:

> For according to Theophrastus a jest is a concealed rebuke for error. Consequently the listener supplies mentally on his own what is missing, just as if he knows and believes it.[18]

This succinct definition of comedy provides, in effect, the theoretical basis for the *Characters*. To demonstrate this, it is helpful to analyse each element of the definition in turn.

The first element is the notion of an 'error', which can be translated as a 'missing of the mark' or 'misjudgement'. This concept appears frequently in Aristotle's ethical writings, and it refers to a failure to judge a situation correctly and to engage in the right conduct that is called for in the circumstances.[19] The term is also used in Aristotle's definition of the ludicrous in the *Poetics*.[20] Theophrastus' character portraits are replete with examples of these sorts of 'errors'. Indeed, one could say that inappropriate, poorly judged, or ill-timed conduct constitutes the core of the work. The *Tactless Man*, for example, brings a higher bidder just after the goods have been sold (12.8–9) or comes to have a discussion when one is exceedingly busy (12.2–3). This concept of 'error' also explains why Theophrastus only focusses on negative aspects of behaviour in the *Characters*, since in his view, it is only erroneous forms of behaviour that can be comical.

The second element of the definition is the 'concealed rebuke'. The reason why the rebuke must be concealed is to distinguish between open, direct insults (which cause pain) and comic jests or gibes (which mask criticism with comic humour and are therefore harmless).[21] In a similar way, Aristotle drew a careful distinction between direct abuse and playful remarks that employ innuendo.[22] Theophrastus' character portraits are, in effect, a set of 'concealed rebukes'. We observe the failure of the characters to accord with societal norms and expectations. Our amusement involves an implied criticism of the behaviour as inappropriate or defective in some way. Comedy helps to conceal or soften this criticism, but it does not remove it.

The third element of the definition is Theophrastus' assertion that "the listener supplies mentally on his own what is missing, just as if he knows and believes it." This statement provides an important insight into Theophrastus' appreciation of audience psychology.[23] Theophrastus is well aware that an audience experiences more pleasure when they are left to discern some things for themselves.[24] When criticism is implied, rather than overtly stated, an audience will perceive the criticism, make independent conclusions and be persuaded by them. In this sense, the speaker/writer has a fairly minimal role; he/she simply lays out the evidence.

This 'minimalist' approach to comedy exactly reflects Theophrastus' methodology in the *Characters*. Theophrastus sets down examples of behaviour with the bare minimum of detail and description and lets the audience judge the inappropriateness of them. The simple descriptions allow us to imagine further aspects of the narrative for ourselves, and the lack of analysis and commentary makes the character portraits enjoyable because we are left to discern the implied ethical lesson for ourselves. The artfulness of the character descriptions lies in the fact that we are led towards a critical outlook without having the criticism explicitly enunciated.

Comedy and the *Characters*

Theophrastus' caricatures are humorous because the characters are unaware of the absurdity and inappropriateness of their behaviour. The *Country Bumpkin*, for example, talks in a bellowing voice and stomps into the Assembly wearing over-sized shoes (4.2) and the *Self-Centred Man* turns back to curse at the stone he has just stumbled over in the street (15.8). The *Obsequious Man* embraces people with both arms and won't let go (5.2); the *Distrustful Man* makes his slave walk in front of him to check that he doesn't run away (18.8); the *Penny-Pincher* turns the house upside down looking for a lost coin (10.6); and the *Tactless Man* serenades his girlfriend when she has a fever (12.3–4). In all of these examples, the characters fail to modify their behaviour according to what is appropriate in the circumstances.

Theophrastus' style of writing enhances the effectiveness of his humour. Theophrastus presents examples of behaviour in short, clipped sentences without elaboration or explanation that would interrupt the descriptive flow or reduce the comic impact. The comic momentum builds rapidly with the use of conjunctions such as 'and', 'then' and 'next'. This style can clearly be seen in the description of the *Chatterbox*:

> Then, as things are going well, he continues with talk like this; people nowadays are far less well-behaved than in the old days; and wheat is selling in the market at a bargain price; and the city is full of foreigners; and the festival of Dionysus heralds the start of the sailing season; and more rain would be good for the crops; and what land he will cultivate next year; and life is hard; and Damippos set up a very large torch at the mysteries; and how many pillars there are in the Odeion; and "I threw up yesterday.
>
> (3.3)

The sudden transition from reported speech to quoted speech in the last line is unexpected and serves as a type of comic punchline.[25]

Theophrastus also uses popular speech in his character portraits. This reflects Theophrastus' broader interest in proverbial sayings, a subject on which he wrote a treatise.[26] The *Obtuse Man* misquotes a saying by commenting on how sweet the 'stars' smell when it rains rather than the 'earth' (14.12–13).[27] The *Disagreeable Man* uses a popular expression by referring to his house as an 'inn' because "it is always full" of visitors (20.9), but he then adds that "his friends are a leaking jar" because, no matter how much hospitality he shows them, he cannot fill them up (20.9–10). The combination of allusion and comic explanation is highly effective and is typical of both popular speech and comedy.[28] In other sketches, Theophrastus changes the context in which formulaic language is used in order to achieve humour.[29] For example, the *Superstitious Man* approaches an official adviser on matters of purification and inquires "what he should do" (16.6) about a trivial matter (a mouse that has nibbled a hole in a sack of barley).

The inclusion of vulgar references to sex, alcohol and personal hygiene adds to the humour of the sketches[30] and is a familiar device from ancient Greek comedy.[31] For example, the *Slanderer* is appropriately crude and vulgar for his type, giving explicit descriptions of the activities of a brothel: "[t]hese women grab passers-by off the street," "[t]his is a house with its legs in the air," and, "they couple in the streets like dogs" (28.3–4).[32] The *Repulsive Man* deliberately lifts up his clothes to expose himself in front of noble women (11.2), he hires a couple of flute-girls and invites passers-by to join him at a symposium (11.8), and he announces in public that he intends to get drunk (11.9). The *Offensive Man* wipes his nose while eating, scratches himself while sacrificing and discharges spit from his mouth while talking (19.5). The *Obtuse Man* is bitten by his neighbour's dog when visiting the toilet at night (14.5) and the *Disagreeable Man* puts everyone off their meal by comparing the colour of blood-broth soup to his bowel motion the night before (20.6).

Although some early editors found the *Characters* a little too frank and vulgar, these judgements often reflect the moral standards of the editor and his/her particular era. The British classicist, Sir Richard Claverhouse Jebb, for example, in his elegant commentary on the *Characters* published in 1870, heavily edited the sketch of the *Offensive Man* on the grounds of impropriety, reducing its length by half.[33] Jebb also edited details of the sketches of the *Slanderer*, the *Country Bumpkin* and the *Late Learner*, removing details which, by modern standards, are fairly innocuous.[34]

Despite Jebb's judgement of some of Theophrastus' subjects as "grotesque",[35] he nevertheless found Theophrastus' humour appealing. Jebb states that Theophrastus' sketches are written with "a good deal of humour and acuteness"[36] and "as if their principal aim was to amuse".[37] Later editors have also expressed an appreciation of the comic aspects of the *Characters*, although they have defined the style of comedy in different ways. Ussher sees in the *Characters* "that touch of the bawdy so ingrained in Aristophanic drama".[38] Rusten and Cunningham state that some of the sketches "quite obviously have comic affinities".[39] Trenkner sees parallels between episodes in the *Characters* and "Aesopean γελοῖα [jokes] and other anecdotes",[40] while Millett sees in them a form of caricature that is based on "blending realism with elements of distortion".[41] Admittedly, there are some occasions where the humour is obscure[42] or the customs referred to are unknown,[43] but, for the most part, the humour in the *Characters* is both effective and recognisable.[44]

As for the role of humour in Theophrastus' teaching, Pasquali has suggested that perhaps Theophrastus wrote the *Characters* for his own amusement or as comic episodes to enliven his lectures on serious topics.[45] Diggle concurs with Pasquali's suggestion and imagines Theophrastus 'acting out' his comic descriptions of types in the course of lectures.[46] In my view, Theophrastus' use of comedy in the *Characters* helped in the delivery of ethical teaching, by presenting the subject of ethics in a practical and appealing way. Theophrastus may well have 'acted out' his character portraits as Diggle suggests, but he did not do this exclusively for the purpose of entertainment. The behaviour of the character types provokes what George Meredith termed "thoughtful laughter".[47] To begin with, an audience will laugh and shake their heads at the inappropriate behaviour of the character types, but soon after, an audience will reflect more deeply on that behaviour and why it is inappropriate in the circumstances, and that is the point at which comedy and ethics intersect.

Keeping this connection between comedy and ethics in mind, we may now consider three questions of particular interest. Firstly, how did the *Characters* fit in with the broader research interests of the Peripatos and, in turn, how did these interests impact upon the comic theatre of the day? Secondly, what similarities are there between the techniques of Theophrastus as a character writer and his student, the comic playwright Menander? Thirdly, what is the effect of Theophrastus' humour on an audience?

The *Characters*, the Peripatos and the comic theatre of Athens

When Theophrastus was composing his character portraits probably in the late fourth century, theatrical festivals were a major feature of religious life in Athens.[48] Aside from tragedies, theatre goers could watch between three and five comedies at the spring festival of the Great Dionysia and a further three to five comedies at the winter festival of the Lenaea.[49] In c. 330 BCE, the new Lycurgan theatre in Athens was completed.[50] This was a testament to Athens' need to accommodate larger audiences as well as its determination to retain primacy of place among the dramatic festival venues.[51] It is likely that most of the male citizens of Athens attended these dramatic festivals, as well as a sizeable contingent of *metics*, foreigners and slaves.[52] The festivals were busy, noisy and bustling events, even during the performances themselves. The Athenian audience was "far from passive. It clapped and shouted approval. If it was not satisfied it whistled, clucked, and banged its heels against the wooden seats. Sometimes it forced a drama to withdraw from the competition." [53] The challenge for a comic poet was to tap into this spirit of revelry and turn it to his advantage.[54]

As a long-term resident of Athens and a keen observer of human behaviour, it is unlikely that Theophrastus would have missed the dramatic festivals which would have represented valuable opportunities to observe the conduct and reactions of his fellow citizens. Theophrastus wrote a work *On Festivals*[55] and makes a number of allusions to the theatre in his character portraits. Taken collectively, the references to the theatre in Theophrastus' *Characters* can even be read as a type of guide to theatre etiquette. From the *Characters*, we learn that it was considered 'shabby' to go to the theatre only when admission was free (30.6–7). It was considered 'repulsive' to applaud when no one else was applauding, to hiss at good actors or to burp loudly in the silent theatre (11.3). It was considered 'shameless' not to pay for all the tickets when attending the theatre with interstate guests (9.5–6) and it was considered 'obtuse' to fall asleep and be left behind alone in the theatre (14.4–5).[56] Given Theophrastus' keen interest in comedy, we can easily imagine Theophrastus attending the theatre both to watch plays and to observe the audience.

Apart from studying and writing works on the subject of comedy, however, Theophrastus was also writing on a multitude of topics directly related to ethics and character.[57] In turn, these studies were connected with a new area of interest being pursued by Theophrastus in his philosophical school: physiognomy.[58] This pseudo-science was based on the premise that a person's character can be deduced from his/her physical appearance.[59] Aristotle had previously written that: "it is possible to infer character from physical features"[60] and the pseudo-Aristotelian treatise known as the *Physiognomonica* states that there is a direct correlation between a permanent physical attribute and a permanent quality of character.[61] The *Physiognomonica* states that the clearest indication of character comes from the eyes, forehead, head and face,[62] but other aspects of the body can also be indicative of character, including movements, gestures, hair, skin and voice.[63]

Theophrastus wrote works that are suggestive of physiognomic interests, particularly his works *On (Types of) Hair*,[64] *On Old Age*[65] and *On the Intelligence and Habits of Living Creatures*.[66] In the context of rhetorical performance, he is reported to have emphasised facial expression and, in particular, the expression of the eyes, as suggested by the following passage:

> [E]verything depends on the face, and in this the entire mastery belongs to the eyes. . . . For delivery is entirely concerned with the soul, and facial expression is an image of the soul, (and) the eyes informants. For this is the one part of the body which can produce as many signs and changes as there are (e)motions of the soul.[67]

There is also an affinity between the 'science' of physiognomy and Theophrastus' *Characters*.[68] The *Physiognomonica*, for example, lists twenty character traits and temperaments (including opposing pairs, such as the Brave Man and Coward, and several single types) with a description of the physical indicators that accompany them.[69] Several of the negative character traits mirror those found in the *Characters*, such as the *Coward*, the *Obtuse Man* and the *Dissembler*.[70]

In the *Characters*, facial features are not a major focus,[71] however, Theophrastus does consider other physical attributes to be indicators of character, especially a person's hair and skin type.[72] Some of Theophrastus' character sketches are replete with physiognomic details, such as the *Offensive Man*:

> The Offensive Man is the kind who parades about with scaly and blanched skin and black nails. . . . He is quite apt to have sores on his shins and lesions on his toes, and instead of treating them he lets them fester. His armpits are infested with lice and their hair extends over much of his sides, and his teeth are black and rotten.

(19.2–5)

Another example is the *Oligarchic Man* who struts about at midday with his hair trimmed and his nails carefully pared (26.4), and an unnamed type who "has frequent haircuts" and "keeps his teeth white" (5.6).

Apart from hair style and skin type, the 'science' of physiognomy held that expressions, movement, gesture and speech could also be important indicators of character.[73] In the *Characters*, facial expressions are occasionally mentioned. For example, the *Rumour-Monger* smiles (disingenuously) when inquiring about his friend's health (8.2), the *Country Bumpkin* stops and stares in wonder at a passing ox, donkey or goat (4.5), and the *Obtuse Man*'s face 'darkens' and bursts into tears before he wishes his dead friend the best of luck (14.7–8). Movements can also be indicative of character: the *Arrogant Man* keeps his head down to avoid making eye contact with passers-by and only looks up when it suits him (24.8); the *Superstitious Man* shudders and spits into his chest when he sees a madman or epileptic (16.15); and the *Late Learner* does frequent buttock-twists so that he might pass for a wrestling expert (27.14).

Certain gestures can also be indicative of character. The *Toady*, for example, pays excessive attention to his host's appearance by 'picking' off lint and straw from his cloak and hair (2.3). The *Shameless Man* laughs and 'snatches' up a free sample from the butcher's table (9.4–5). The *Penny-Pincher* 'dives' after the rubbish looking for a lost penny (10.7) and the *Repulsive Man* 'raises' his head up high to burp in the silent theatre (11.3). Different types of voice also feature in the *Characters*. The *Man Who Has Lost All Sense* rails at crowds in a 'loud, cracked voice' (6.7), while the *Country Bumpkin* talks in a booming voice (4.2–3).[74]

Theophrastus' interests in physiognomy and character are likely to have directly influenced the development of 'signifiers' of character on the comic stage.[75] Although character types, such as the rustic slave, were a prominent feature of earlier comedy,[76] particularly in the plays of Aristophanes (446–386 BCE), the fourth century saw a further development of 'stock' characters.[77] Also in the late fourth century, comic masks evolved from the simple grotesque masks of earlier comedy which tended to depict the ugly or elderly, to more sophisticated masks representing a whole range of character types, including "the soldier, young lover, strict father, rustic, *hetaira* [prostitute], pimp, parasite, flatterer, cook and cunning slave".[78] For each character type, a set of features on the mask including hair type, the shape of the eyes, the character of the eyebrows, the beard, the fullness of the cheeks and the shape of the lips, pointed to particular behavioural characteristics along with the character's costume and props.[79]

In effect, the physical features of comic masks became a shorthand method for portraying character in a more realistic way.[80] The Rustic Youth, for example, was dark-skinned to indicate that he worked outdoors, with thick lips to indicate stupidity and a snub nose to indicate lasciviousness.[81] In contrast, the Delicate Youth wore a festive wreath, with white skin to indicate effeminacy and soft, chubby cheeks to indicate a soft lifestyle.[82] The features of the mask helped the audience to recognise the basic character type and to make certain assumptions about that type's likely behavioural traits.

Importantly, however, the development of masks with distinctive facial features did not lead to a bland and predictable approach to the presentation of character traits on the comic stage.[83] Just as in Theophrastus' *Characters*, modes of speech, gestures and movements added complexity and individuality to the basic type that was indicated by the mask.[84] Sometimes, comic playwrights would deliberately disprove assumptions so that the typically boastful and arrogant soldier, for example, would prove by means of his speech and conduct to be genuinely soft-hearted and deeply in love.[85] In this way, fourth-century comedy played with audience expectations about character types, introducing nuances into characterisation in order to enrich a particular type.[86] Comic playwrights took basic character types as their starting point, but the dialogue and action of the play added further dimensions to those types. In the *Characters*, Theophrastus portrays many subtle and complex character cues, as indicated by gestures, modes of speech and behaviour. This sort of nuanced study of character would have been very useful to students seeking to merge the study of physiognomy with the presentation of character in the comic theatre, combining the use of masks as basic indicators of character, with gesture and speech as more complex indicators of character.

There is also a direct similarity between the realistic setting of Theophrastus' character portraits and the increased emphasis on everyday settings in the comic plays of the fourth century. In the *Characters*, Theophrastus situates his character types in an everyday Athenian setting to show how they interact with fellow citizens, friends and family.[87] The realistic depictions of public and private spaces in the city of Athens form a type of stage and backdrop for Theophrastus' *Characters*. Similarly, in the comic theatre of the late fourth century, there is a marked emphasis on a realistic reproduction of Athenian daily life with carefully crafted characters caught up in domestic intrigues, rather than myth, politics, and fabulous schemes and plots.[88] For this reason, the comedy of the late fourth century has been described as a "private comedy of manners",[89] a description that equally befits Theophrastus' *Characters*.

Theophrastus' *Characters* can therefore be viewed as a product of Theophrastus' interest in comedy combined with his interest in ethics, character and physiognomy. This multidisciplinary approach was typical of Theophrastus' studies at the Peripatos. In the *Characters*, Theophrastus adopted comedy to suit his own purposes and to engage his audience on the subject of ethics. But Theophrastus' approach was also influential outside of the Peripatos. In particular, Theophrastus' identification of fixed character traits, and his careful delineation of character types using physical signs, modes of speech, gesture and movement, would have been especially helpful to those learning the art of characterisation[90] and applying it to the comic stage.[91] A direct line of influence from the Peripatos to the Athenian comic theatre can be seen most clearly in the works of the comic playwright Menander.

Theophrastus and Menander

The master of the 'character' play of the fourth century was Menander.[92] Born in Athens c. 342 BCE,[93] and the son of a wealthy Athenian, Menander first learned the art of writing plays from Alexis, a major comic playwright of the period.[94] Later, he was taught by Theophrastus at the Peripatos in Athens.[95] Theophrastus and Menander were both friends and acquaintances of the Athenian leader Demetrius of Phalerum (also a former student of Theophrastus).[96] When Theophrastus was writing his *Characters*, probably around 319 BCE, Menander was just making his name as a comic dramatist. Menander's first play was entitled *Wrath* and it won first prize in the dramatic contest of 322/321 BCE.[97] The *Bad-Tempered Man*, for which Menander won first prize at the Greater Dionysia in 316 BCE, is the best-preserved play by Menander and a brilliant character portrait of a misanthropic old farmer.

As a playwright, Menander proved to be highly skilled at presenting human behaviour in dramatic form. But the influence of Menander's education at the Peripatos no doubt contributed to this success.[98] Theophrastus' keen observations of people's behaviour, mannerisms and modes of speech; precision in demarcating character traits and presenting them in a realistic setting; and wit and humour all very likely influenced Menander. If Theophrastus described, and even mimicked, character types during his lectures, as some have suggested,[99] then Menander would have benefited from witnessing Theophrastus' character acting. Undoubtedly, Menander went on to refine and perfect his skills in characterisation as a playwright, but it is nonetheless likely that, as a student, Menander learned "his subtlety in typological analysis in the school of Theophrastus".[100]

In support of this view, we can see direct parallels between the character sketches of Theophrastus and the titles of Menander's plays.[101] Theophrastus' sketch of the *Self-Centred Man* in the *Characters*, for example, seems like a direct precursor to Menander's *Bad-Tempered Man* since both types are gruff, grumpy, unsociable and uncooperative. And there are four other character types in Theophrastus' *Characters* that share their names with titles of fragmentary plays by Menander: namely, the *Country Bumpkin*, the *Distrustful Man*, the *Superstitious Man*, and the *Flatterer*. Surviving titles of Menandrian plays also evoke Theophrastus' interest in negative behavioural traits, such as the *False-accuser*, the *Woman-Hater*, and the *Hated Man*.[102] Although Theophrastus usually focusses on behavioural traits, his portraits of 'social' and 'professional' types in the *Characters* reflect the stock types of Menandrian comedy, such as Theophrastus' sketches of the *Flatterer* (the professional parasite), the *Country Bumpkin* (or Rustic), the *Oligarchic Man* and the *Friend of Villains*.[103] As Segal summarises, "Theophrastus' vignettes seem like sketches for Menandrian men and women."[104]

The titles of Menander's plays indicate that he, like Theophrastus, was skilled in portraying human behaviour and had a particular interest in human failings and character weaknesses.[105] Theophrastus pursues this interest with a gentle humour and, although he portrays only negative traits in the *Characters*, he does not portray genuinely evil or degraded types.[106] In a similar way, Menander is careful to portray types that are not morally repulsive.[107] In the *Bad-Tempered Man*, for example, the protagonist Knemon is cantankerous and unfriendly. Yet, he attracts some sympathy when he explains the hardships he has undergone, and his simple desire to be isolated from a world of troubles:

> I'd like to tell you one/Or two things [about] me and my ways. If everyone behaved/[Like me, we should have] no law-courts, shouldn't send each other to/Prison, [and] there'd be [no] wars. Each man would have enough to live/On, and he'd be satisfied.[108]

In the *Characters*, Theophrastus explores a range of traits and behaviours that are habitual and ingrained, but generally avoidable through the proper exercise of practical wisdom. In the following fragment, Menander comments on certain character weaknesses as self-inflicted, even making reference to one of Theophrastus' character portraits:

> [W]e, over and above our inevitable troubles/ourselves provide additional ones of our own making./We're annoyed, if someone sneezes. If someone abuses us,/we become angry. If someone has a dream,/we become quite frightened. If an owl calls out, we get nervous./Our stresses, imaginings, ambitions, customs/Are all above and beyond the troubles from nature.[109]

Menander's description of the man who is frightened by a dream or feels nervous upon hearing an owl very closely resembles Theophrastus' description of the *Superstitious Man* who has a troubling dream (16.11) and becomes agitated upon hearing the screeching of an owl (16.8).

Apart from a shared interest in subject matter, there are several important similarities in Theophrastus' and Menander's methodology. The first is an ability to convey character with precision and minimal detail, exemplifying behavioural traits through the use of quoted speech and without any detailed examination of underlying motives or intentions.[110] In the *Characters*, Theophrastus uses quoted speech to allow his characters to speak for themselves,[111] such as in Theophrastus' description of the *Slanderer*:

> You can be sure that when he hears others talking slanderously he will join in with 'There's nobody I detest more than that man. He's got a repulsive face. And his depravity has no equal. I tell you: his wife brought him a dowry of a talent, but since she presented him with a child he has given her only threepence a day for food and he makes her wash in cold water during the month of Poseidon.'

> (28.4–5)

Theophrastus' use of quoted speech brings a certain 'dramatic' quality to the character portrait, creating an impression that the character is speaking directly to the reader without interference or judgement from the author.[112]

In a similar way, Menander relies heavily on quoted speech, which is indicative of his view that "the stamp of a man is recognised from his speech."[113] Even in the case of very minor characters who are assigned very few lines of speech, Menander manages to create memorable character types. This is the case with the young maiden Myrrhine, the daughter of Knemon in the *Bad-Tempered Man*:

> I'm so unhappy, oh, it's all gone wrong!/What am I going to do now? Nurse was hauling up/The bucket, and she dropped it in the well![114]

In just a few lines, Menander successfully conveys a vivid impression of Myrrhine's helplessness, simplicity and charming naiveté.

Theophrastus often compresses several examples of quoted speech into a single episode, thereby exaggerating the character trait in question. In the sketch of the

Dissembler, for example, the expressions typically used by this character type demonstrate his tendency to feign disbelief:

> In general he is a great one for using expressions like 'I don't believe it', 'I can't imagine it', 'I am amazed' . . . . 'But *that* was not the account he gave me', 'It beggars belief', 'Tell that to someone else', 'I don't know whether I should disbelieve *you* or condemn *him*', 'Are you sure you are not being too credulous?'
>
> (1.6)

In a similar way, Menander relies on exaggerated and dramatic dialogue to reveal character.[115] Knemon, for example, is described as a misanthropic old grouch long before he appears on stage. When Knemon finally makes an entrance, his opening monologue, which is full of bitter complaints about humanity, confirms all the earlier reports about his character:

> Well, wasn't that Perseus such a lucky fellow,/On two accounts? He had some wings, and so/Didn't meet any pedestrians on the ground./And then he owned a sort of instrument/With which he petrified all who annoyed him!/I wish *I* had one now! Then nothing would/Be commoner all over than stone statues![116]

In instances where character types share similar traits, such as loquacity, Theophrastus carefully differentiates between them through their manner of speech. Theophrastus' *Chatterbox*, for example, talks endlessly about trivial and unrelated matters, while the *Talker* thinks he is an authority on every subject, and the *Rumour-Monger* fabricates news and lies about his sources. Similarly, in Menander's plays, stock characters are carefully differentiated from one another through their modes of speech. In the *Bad-Tempered Man*, for example, three of Menander's stock characters represent different positions on the spectrum of 'friendliness'.[117] Sikon the cook is an obsequious flatterer who flatters others in order to get his own way,[118] Gorgias is friendly and speaks with reason and due measure,[119] while Knemon is very unfriendly and speaks rudely and aggressively.[120]

As we have already noted, Theophrastus relies on a realistic and everyday setting as a backdrop for his character types. In Theophrastus' *Characters*, the backdrop is fourth-century Athens, with scenes from the marketplace, law courts, assembly, bathhouse and theatre. The public venues of Athens become a kaleidoscopic and moving stage for Theophrastus' characters, and by skipping between different scenes and settings, Theophrastus maintains interest and engagement. But Theophrastus also includes insights into the conduct of his characters in private and domestic contexts which were normally closed to public view.[121] This makes the audience feel especially privileged and opens up new opportunities for comedy. So, for example, Theophrastus relates the following episode about the *Distrustful Man*:

> While lying in bed he asks his wife whether she has closed the chest and sealed the sideboard and whether the front door has been bolted, and if she

says yes he throws off the bedclothes anyway and gets up with nothing on and lights the lamp and runs around in his bare feet to inspect everything in person, and so he hardly gets any sleep.

(18.4–5)

The absurdity of the *Distrustful Man's* behaviour becomes even more pronounced against the intimate and everyday backdrop.[122] In Menander's plays too, the setting is typically simple and domestic, focussing on neighbouring households in rural Attica or in cities such as Athens or Corinth.[123] Like the setting of the *Characters*, the familiar and everyday setting in Menander's plays helps to focus attention on the particular character traits and modes of behaviour.

One of the most striking features of Menander's surviving work is the combination of ethics and comedy in his plays, and in particular his love of philosophising.[124] This is an entirely logical result of Menander's education under Theophrastus at the Peripatos.[125] Menander's characters often express principles of philosophical wisdom and, on occasion, they undergo processes of moral reformation. A good example is Knemon in the *Bad-Tempered Man* who, after being retrieved from a well, realises that he cannot afford to be so dismissive of his friends and neighbours. He then delivers a philosophical monologue in which he sets out his reformed views about the value of friendship:

One mistake, perhaps, I *did* make – I believed that I was the/One man in the world who could be self-contained, and wouldn't require/Help from any man. However, I've seen now that death can strike/Suddenly and with no warning, and I've realised that my/Past belief was wrong. You always need someone who'll lend a hand,/Someone on the doorstep.[126]

This tendency in Menander's work reflects Theophrastus' teaching and writings on ethical subjects, especially his interest in character, fate and friendship.[127] As Ireland has observed, "time and again throughout the plays, there is evidence of an ethos and approach to life that clearly points to the teachings of the Lyceum in general (most notably Aristotelian ethics) and what little we know of Theophrastus in particular."[128]

To be sure, Menander's plays are not philosophical treatises,[129] but there are striking similarities between the sorts of philosophical topics in which Theophrastus and Menander are interested. One example is the notion of character as dependent upon ethical conduct.[130] Theophrastus and Menander shared a common interest in the role of character in human behaviour.[131] Theophrastus, like Aristotle, viewed character as a quality that needs to be maintained through virtuous conduct in order to achieve happiness.[132] At the same time, Theophrastus took a practical approach: he was not naïve about the difficulties of always being virtuous and he is recorded as saying that although it is difficult to evaluate and to choose the best life, it is much more difficult to remain on that path after selecting it.[133] In *The Arbitration*, Menander presents a similar view of character as a type of internal and divine guardian that responds to one's choices; if a person makes a good choice, he/she achieves happiness, but if a person makes a bad choice, he/she suffers for it and someone else benefits. Like Theophrastus, Menander appears to have seen character and ethical behaviour as the chief determinants of whether happiness is ultimately attained:

> They['ve introduced],/As each man's guardian, his character./Inside us, it's [on duty (?)] – *damns* us if/[We treat] it badly, *guards* the others. That's/Our god, responsible for failure and/Success in each of us. To get on well,/You must placate it by avoiding error and/Stupidity![134]

In addition, both Theophrastus and Menander appear to have held the view that misfortune in life can lead to a loss of virtue.[135] Aristotle held a different view: in his opinion, the life of virtue and contemplation leads to a self-sufficient happiness which cannot be undermined by external events.[136] In contrast, Theophrastus stated that wisdom and virtue are not sufficient to guarantee a happy life because misfortune can lead to a loss of virtue.[137] Unfortunate states, such as grief, sickness and poverty can interfere with a happy life and these are matters over which an individual has no control.[138] Cicero reports that Theophrastus was widely criticised by other philosophers for this view and for praising the maxim that "Fortune rules life, not wisdom."[139] Other philosophers apparently viewed this stance as 'faint-hearted' yet Theophrastus maintained that misfortune has the power to make life miserable[140] and this view is recorded in more than one ancient sourc.[141]

In three fragments from separate plays, Menander reflects similar views to Theophrastus on the supremacy of fortune (or chance). In Menander's play *The Shield*, the personification of Chance alludes to her ability to cause difficulties and to reveal a person's true character:

> He'll cause himself much toil and trouble, show/His true colours more clearly to the world,/And then go back to where he was before./I've still to tell you who I am, the steward/And judge controlling all this. I'm called Chance.[142]

In a fragment of Menander's *Mercenary Recruiter*, an unknown character comments on the irrationality of chance:

> any benefit there is in human life/is brought about by chance, completely unexpectedly./She doesn't use rules to make her decisions/and it's impossible for any man alive to say "*that* will never happen to me."[143]

Similarly, in a fragment from Menander's *Spurious Child*, the following lines appear:

> Stop trying to be sensible: human sense/is no help, it's the sense of chance,/whether this is the divine spirit or an intelligence,/it is this that directs and saves and governs/everything, while human forethought is smoke/and nonsense. Be persuaded, and don't blame me;/everything we intend or say or do/ is chance, and we just claim credit for it.[144]

In sum, it is very likely that, as Theophrastus' student, Menander received instruction on the subjects of ethics, comedy and character at the Peripatos and that he owes some debt to Theophrastus for developing his skills in characterisation.[145] Theophrastus' ability to carefully identify and describe different types of character is likely to have been particularly useful to Menander as a budding playwright. The value of an everyday and realistic setting to highlight character qualities may also have influenced Menander's choice of setting. Menander even reflects the influence of Theophrastus' ethical teachings in his dramatic dialogues. This is more than just an 'affinity of outlook'.[146] Both Theophrastus and Menander recognised that the combination of ethics and comedy was effective, entertaining and meaningful and would appeal to a wider audience than might be reached by either comedy or ethics alone.

The effect of comedy in the *Characters*

There is little doubt that the combination of comedy and ethics in the *Characters* is highly effective in terms of conveying ethical teaching in an engaging and practical way. In the following discussion, we will consider the effect of Theophrastus' 'thoughtful laughter' on his audience. What did Theophrastus intend for his audience to take away from laughing at the character types he described? I will suggest two possible answers: firstly, an increase in self-awareness and, secondly, a form of comic catharsis.

One of the main targets of Theophrastus' humour in the *Characters* is a lack of self-awareness. This concept has its origins in Platonic philosophy in which Socrates defines the comic as a lack of self-awareness that may manifest itself in one of three ways; either in the belief that one is richer, or more beautiful, or more virtuous (and often wiser) than is the case.[147] In Theophrastus' *Characters*, we unmistakably witness a variety of forms of self-ignorance which, in turn, provoke laughter. The *Late Learner* believes that he is younger and fitter than he actually is, taking part in torch-races and beauty contests (27.4,8). The *Oligarchic Man* believes that he is superior to ordinary people, but he knows only one line of Homer (26.2). The *Boastful Man* claims that he served with Alexander the Great on campaign although he has never left the city (23.3–4).

Theophrastus takes this further and demonstrates that there are a myriad of other forms of poor self-awareness, including the belief that one is more interesting than one is (the *Chatterbox*), better informed (the *Rumour-Monger*), more capable (the *Overzealous Man*) and more important (the *Man of Petty Ambition*, the *Boastful Man*, the *Arrogant Man*). He even introduces a new category of ignorance based on a mistaken conviction that one is *less* fortunate than is actually the case (as seen in the sketch of the *Ungrateful Grumbler* and the *Superstitious Man*). In all of these sketches, the lack of self-awareness is worthy of laughter because the characters fail to recognise and address failings in themselves that are readily apparent to others.[148]

After witnessing all these forms of inappropriate behaviour in the *Characters*, and laughing at their lack of self-awareness, one inevitably becomes more sensitised to appropriate conduct in social interaction.[149] The process of laughing at certain forms of behaviour affirms and strengthens underlying social opinions about proper behaviour.[150] Through laughing at character types that neglect to worship the gods, for example, or are overly afraid of the influence of the gods, the underlying norm of proper devotion to the gods is strengthened and any inclination to either extreme is censured. Acts that deviate from social norms (both serious and trivial) incur ridicule, such as avoiding paying for a theatre ticket (9.5) or contributing to a collection (22.9). Through observing and ridiculing characters who defy these social conventions, the conventions themselves are confirmed to be important.[151] In this way, the comic dimension of the *Characters* is closely tied to the reinforcement of appropriate social conduct.[152]

On an individual level also, the *Characters* has the potential to enhance our awareness *of our own* traits and characteristic forms of speech and behaviour. If we had to identify a type that most closely resembles us, which type would it be? Do we behave, or have we ever behaved, in the same way as any of the character types described? It can be an uncomfortable experience to recognise elements of the characters in oneself, such as the reluctance of the *Penny-Pincher* to lend items to others (10.13), or the stupidity of the *Obtuse Man* in adding too much salt to his dinner (14.11), or the willingness of the *Overzealous Man* to take others on a shortcut only to find himself lost (13.6–7). Yet, the heightened self-awareness that is prompted by Theophrastus' analysis of negative character traits is arguably a healthy and desirable outcome.

If Theophrastus is targeting a lack of self-awareness with his comedy, what effect does laughing at these types have on the audience? It is well known, for example, that Aristotle introduced the concept of the 'cathartic' effect of tragedy, in 'bringing to an end' pity and fear and similar emotions.[153] On the subject of comedy, however, Aristotle was less forthcoming. The *Poetics* states summarily:

> Comedy, as we said, is mimesis of baser but not wholly vicious characters: rather, the laughable is one category of the shameful. For the laughable comprises any fault or mark of shame which involves no pain or destruction.[154]

The behaviours of Theophrastus' character types certainly fit this definition of comedy by representing actions that are base and shameful; for example, the *Penny-Pincher* who won't let anyone eat fallen fruit from his orchard (10.8), the *Illiberal Man* who pretends that his children are ill so that he can avoid paying a school contribution (22.6), and the *Superstitious Man* who must wash his hands three times, sprinkle himself with holy water and put a laurel leaf in his mouth before leaving the house each day (16.2).

Is it possible that, in laughing at these types, Theophrastus intended for his audience to experience a type of "comic catharsis" whereby laughter expurgates certain emotions and, if so, which emotions?[155] The concept of comic catharsis has been hotly debated.[156] Fortenbaugh suggests that the object of comedy may be to generate laughter by giving it repeated release so that one can then return to functioning in a serious and well-organised manner.[157] This certainly helps to explain *how* comedy functions as a type of release, but it does not describe *which* emotions are purged by comedy.

It is possible that the sorts of emotions being targeted by Theophrastus are annoyance, contempt and intolerance. In everyday life, an encounter with a type such as the *Chatterbox*, an *Arrogant Man* or a *Toady* might reasonably provoke any or all of these emotions.[158] In fact, this is confirmed by some emotional responses recorded in the text of the *Characters* itself. The *Shameless Man*, for example, ignores the bath attendant and douses himself with water, and in response the bath attendant shouts out in angry protest (9.8). Similarly, when the *Late Learner* falls in love with a prostitute and rams her door, the prostitute's other lover tracks him down and beats him up (27.9). When the *Man Who Has Lost All Sense* demands an entrance fee from people who already hold tickets to a show, he provokes a fight (6.4).

Without the charm of comedy, Theophrastus' characters come across as rude, irritating, disgusting, arrogant and loathsome types that provoke indignation.[159] With the introduction of humour, however, these feelings of irritation and contempt are quelled. Theophrastus thereby encourages us to view irritating character types not with feelings of superiority, disdain, contempt or a "comfortably narrow"[160] viewpoint, but with a humane outlook, emotional distance, a comic appreciation of the incongruities of their behaviour and, perhaps most importantly, an awareness of the potential for similar tendencies in our own behaviour. In other words, the cathartic effect of Theophrastus' comedy leads to a positive change in perspective on our fellow human beings. The result is a kindlier attitude and a comic sympathy for "all the faults, mistakes, traps, and deceptions by which people often complicate their lives".[161] At the same time as making us laugh, Theophrastus hopes to achieve an increase in self-awareness, to appeal to our more civilised qualities and to effect a slight improvement in social values and morals.[162]

Notes

1 Boyce 1967: 177.
2 DL 5.46.184 = fr. 1 = fr. 666, no. 23.
3 DL 5.47.208 = fr. 1 = fr. 666, no. 22.
4 DL 5.47.223 = fr. 1= fr. 666, no. 20.
5 DL 5.47.210 = fr. 1 = fr. 666, no.17a. See Fortenbaugh 2003b: 91.
6 *Gnomologium Vaticanum*, no. 331 = fr. 452. For discussion see Fortenbaugh 2011: 324–27.
7 Plutarch, *Table Talk* 2.1.9 633B = fr. 31. The joke is based on word-play: see Fortenbaugh 2003a: 87–8. For a possible connection with Aristotle's discussion of the snub nose see Aristotle's *Metaphysics* 7.5.2–5 (1030b10–1031a1). My thanks to Han Baltussen for pointing this out. For other jokes attributed to Theophrastus see *Depository of Wisdom Literature* chap. On Theophrastus, saying no. 9 = fr. 474 and discussion in Fortenbaugh 2011: 376–7.
8 Diomedes, *The Art of Grammar* 3, Chapter on Poems = fr. 708.
9 Diomedes, *The Art of Grammar* 3, Chapter on Poems = fr. 708, lines 487–488.
10 The source text is unclear: see Fortenbaugh 2005: 424–5.

11 Athenaeus, *The Sophists at Dinner* 6.79 261D–E = fr. 709.
12 See Athenaeus, *The Sophists at Dinner* 6.79 261D–E, lines 9–10 = fr. 709.
13 See discussion in Fortenbaugh 2003b: 105–6; 2003d: 300–1; and 2003e. For Theophrastus' view on the permanence of bad character traits see Stobaeus, *Anthology* 2.31.124 = fr. 465 and discussion in Fortenbaugh 2011: 355. Pertinent comment also in Halliwell 2008: 20.
14 See Fortenbaugh 2003b: 94–95.
15 Arist. *Po.*1449a32–37, transl. Halliwell (Loeb).
16 For discussion see Halliwell 2008: 326–8. Also Golden 1987: 172ff.
17 See *Gnomologium Vaticanum*, no. 327 = fr. 453.
18 Plutarch, *Table Talk* 2.1.4 631D–E = fr. 711. Discussion in Fortenbaugh 2005: 390–4.
19 *EN* 2.6.12–14 (1106a25–35).
20 See Arist. *Po.* 5 1449a34–5; discussed in Fortenbaugh 2005: 393.
21 See fr. 711, note 1; discussion in Fortenbaugh 2005: 393–4. For a discussion of Aristotle's views on avoiding pain in comedy see Rusten 2014: 37–8.
22 *Rh.* 3.11.6–7 (1412a–b) and *EN* 4.8.5–6 (1128a17–25).
23 Fortenbaugh 2005: 423, 425.
24 For another example of Theophrastus' awareness of audience psychology see Demetrius, *On Style* 222 = fr. 696.
25 On variation between the narrator's and subject's voices see Millett 2007: 117.
26 DL 5.45.148 (*On Proverbs*) = fr. 1 = fr. 727, no. 14.
27 See commentary in Diggle 2004: 340–1.
28 See Diggle 2004: 402.
29 See Diggle 2004: 360.
30 For a discussion of Theophrastean character types speaking in unacceptable ways see Halliwell 2008: 237–43. For comparison with everyday forms of speech used by Menander see Lowe 2007: 65–6. On name calling in Menander's plays see Scafuro 2014b: 226.
31 Ussher 1977: 75.
32 On the use of obscenity, vulgarity and abusive words in Greek comedy see Willi 2002: 10–12.
33 See Millett 2007: 5.
34 For example, the *Country Bumpkin* who sits with his cloak hitched up, revealing his nakedness (4.4) and the *Late Learner*, who rams a prostitute's door (27.9–10).
35 Jebb-Sandys: 17.
36 Jebb-Sandys: 1.
37 Jebb-Sandys: 13.
38 Ussher 1977: 75.
39 Rusten and Cunningham 2002: 16.
40 Trenkner 1958: 149.
41 Millett 2007: 38.
42 We cannot know precisely what is amusing (or inappropriate) about dancing the Cordax sober (6.3) or joining in with a child's game of 'Wineskin' and 'Axe' (5.5), for example.
43 For a survey of some of the unusual customs mentioned in the *Characters* see Hicks 1882.
44 For a discussion of various cultural dissimilarities see Lane Fox 1996: 156–7.
45 Pasquali 1918: 77.
46 Diggle 2004: 15–16.
47 Meredith in Corrigan 1965: 470.
48 Habicht 1997: 99–100.
49 Csapo 2010: 108.
50 Csapo 2010: 107.

51 Csapo 2014: 56; also Scafuro 2014a: 200.
52 On the composition of the audience see Rosivach 2000; on *metics* at the theatre see Roselli 2011: 118ff.
53 Csapo 2014: 55.
54 Csapo 2010: 141–2.
55 DL 5.47.196 = fr. 1 = 580, no.2.
56 See also the *Late Learner* (27.6–7), the *Flatterer* (2. 11–12), and the *Talker* (7.9).
57 See Fortenbaugh 2011: 739–40.
58 See Csapo 2014: 58–9.
59 Porter 2005: 58.
60 Arist. *APr.* 1.70b5 (transl. Barnes).
61 Arist. *Phgn.* 1.806a5–10.
62 Arist. *Phgn.* 6.814b1–5.
63 Arist. *Phgn.* 2.806a20–35.
64 DL 5.45.161 = fr. 1 = 328 no. 13.
65 DL 5.43.88 = fr. 1 = 436 no. 18.
66 DL 5.49.254 = fr. 1 = 350 no. 11. For the overlap between Theophrastus' study of the physiognomy of the human form and that of animals see Porter 2005: 59–60. For a comparison between the changing colour of a cowardly man and an octopus see Plutarch, *Natural Explanations* 19 916B = fr. 365C, and compare Theophrastus' *Coward* (25) and Homer's description of the coward (*Iliad*, 13.278–286) discussed in Chapter Two. Theophrastus' works *On Ways and Characters and Habitats* (fr. 350.12), *On Difference of Voice in Creatures of the Same Kind* (DL 5.43.108), and *On as Many Creatures as are said to be Grudging* (DL 5.43.111) also suggest physiognomic interests.
67 Cicero, *On the Orator* 3.221 = fr. 713.
68 It was this affinity that prompted Frances Howell to produce a series of thirty brilliant physiognomic sketches to accompany his translation of the *Characters of Theophrastus* published in 1824. These sketches are reproduced in Anderson's 1970 edition (see bibliography).
69 See Arist. *Phgn.* 2.807a30–808b10.
70 See Arist. *Phgn.*: the coward at 3.807b5–12, the obtuse man at 3.807b20–29 and the dissembler at 3.808a27–29.
71 Fortenbaugh 2003c: 261.
72 See Porter 2005: 55. In Theophrastus' sketch of the *Rumour-Monger*, he refers to the physically altered faces of the political leaders having witnessed a particularly bloody battle (see 8.8).
73 See Vogt 2006: 264–71.
74 All this seems to contradict Millett's view that physiognomy plays virtually no part in the *Characters*: see Millett 2007: 28.
75 In support of this view see Csapo 2014: 58–9. Also see Wiles 1991: 85.
76 Ussher 1977: 78.
77 Ruffell 2014: 147–8.
78 Scafuro 2014a: 201.
79 Ruffell 2014: 151.
80 Wiles 1991: 68. Ruffell 2014: 160.
81 Csapo 2014: 62.
82 Csapo 2014: 60–2.
83 Wiles 1991: 88.
84 Mc C. Brown 1987: 183.
85 Ruffell 2014: 154–5. Csapo 2014: 60. Also Mc C. Brown 1987: 183.
86 For a discussion of the 'soldier' type in Menander's plays see Goldberg 1980: 110–11.
87 See Lane Fox 1996: 129–30 and Millett 2007: 54.
88 Lape and Moreno 2014: 336.

89   Green 1990: 66. Also see Lape and Moreno 2014: 352.
90   Ussher 1977: 75.
91   See Scafuro 2014b: 234 and Konstan 2014: 292.
92   Hunter 2014: 374–5.
93   Scafuro 2014b: 218.
94   Ireland 2010: 342.
95   DL 5.37.1 = fr. 1. In this fragment, Diogenes is quoting from Pamphila's thirty-second book of the *Commentaries*. Diggle describes this as a 'late and dubious source': Diggle 2004: 8; but even if Menander was not Theophrastus' student in a direct sense (as Pamphila claims), this does not rule out Theophrastus' influence.
96   Menander was nearly put on trial for his connections with Demetrius of Phalerum when the latter was ousted in 307 BC. Demetrius' cousin Telesphorus helped him evade the charge. See DL 5.79.
97   Green 1990: 71.
98   Scholars have not always been willing to recognise Theophrastean influence on Menander. Barigazzi (1965) and Gaiser (1967) were among the first to argue in favour of it (see Casanova 2013: 138). Two decades later, Hunter asserted that it was absurd to suggest any correlation (Hunter 1985: 147ff). Now, this view is softening again. See Segal 2001: xv.
99   Diggle 2004: 15–16.
100 Casanova 2013: 140. Also see Scafuro 2014b: 234.
101 On titles see Diggle 2004: 8.
102 For a list of Menander's plays and fragments of unknown plays see Rusten 2011: 627ff.
103 See Boyce 1967: 7.
104 Segal 2001: xv. Also see Rusten and Cunningham 2002: 16.
105 See Casanova 2013: 140.
106 See Volt 2010: 320.
107 Perry 1968: 47.
108 Men. *Dysk.* 742–45, transl. Arnott (Loeb).
109 Fragment of Menander (uncertain play) quoted in Stobaeus 4.34.7 = fr. 844 in Rusten 2011: 658.
110 See Fortenbaugh 2003d: 296–8.
111 The importance of allowing characters to speak for themselves was recognised by Aristotle in his comments on Homer in the *Poetics* at 1460a5–11. On Menander's use of quoted speech to give a sense of authenticity see Nünlist 2002: 238.
112 In contrast, the intrusive authorial voice detracts from the illusion of realism and reduces the emotional intensity: see Lodge 1992: 10, 128.
113 Menander fr. 72 as quoted in Diggle 2004: 4–5. Diggle discusses how speech characterises Theophrastus' character types on pages 23–4.
114 Men. *Dysk.* 189–91 (transl. Arnott).
115 See Nünlist 2002: 233–47.
116 Men. *Dysk.* 153–9 (transl. Arnott).
117 Haegemans 2001: 695.
118 Men. *Dysk.* 487–99.
119 Men. *Dysk.* 271–88.
120 Men. *Dysk.* 172–9. Discussion in Haegemans 2001: 694–6.
121 See Millett 2007: 80.
122 Other examples of domestic scenes are the *Illiberal Man* sweeping the house and debugging the couches (22.12–13), the *Penny-Pincher* moving the furniture to find a lost coin (10.6) and the *Country Bumpkin* raiding the larder and eating his breakfast while feeding the animals (4.6–9).
123 On the realistic location of Menander's *Dyskolos* see Lowe 2001.

124 See Hunter 2014: 382, Konstan 2014: 292, Fortenbaugh 1974. On the "sophisticated philosophical system" underpinning Menander's plays see Lowe 2007: 72.
125 Cinaglia tries hard to identify similarities between Aristotle's and Menander's thought-world, but a more natural pairing, both logically and chronologically, is surely Theophrastus and Menander. See Cinaglia 2013: 163. Also Casanova 2013: 140.
126 Men. *Dysk.* 713–718, transl. Arnott (Loeb).
127 On Theophrastus' views on friendship, see Chapter Four.
128 Ireland 2010: 360.
129 Ireland 2010: 360. Also Casanova 2013: 142.
130 See De Temmerman 2014: 11.
131 For similarities between Menander's plays and Aristotle's *Nicomachean Ethics* see Fortenbaugh 1974.
132 For Theophrastus' views on virtue see pseudo-Plutarch, *On the Opinions of the Philosophers* 1, Introduction 874F–875A = fr. 479 and Ambrose, *On the Duties of Ministers* 2.2 = fr. 480B.
133 Codex Neapolitanus II D 22, sent. 18 = fr. 476.
134 Men. *Epit.* 1093–2000, transl. Arnott (Loeb).
135 Similar sentiments are expressed by Demetrius of Phalerum in his sayings (see DL 5.82–3 as discussed in Sollenberger 2000: 324).
136 *EN* 1.7.6–8 (1097b8–21).
137 Cicero, *On Ends* 5.12 = fr. 498.
138 See Cicero, *On Ends* 5.77 and 5.85–6 = frs 495 and 496.
139 Cicero, *Tusculan Disputations* 5.24–5 = fr. 493.
140 Cicero, *Tusculan Disputations* 5.24–5 = fr. 493.
141 See Plutarch, *Pericles* 38.1–2 = fr. 463.
142 Men. *Asp.* 144–148, transl. Arnott (Loeb).
143 Fragment of Menander, *Mercenary Recruiter* as quoted in Stobaeus 1.7.7 = fr. 256 in Rusten 2011: 645.
144 Fragment of Menander, *Spurious Child* or *Farmer* in Stobaeus 1.6.1 = fr. 372 in Rusten 2011: 652.
145 See Lane Fox 1996: 140.
146 See Lane Fox 1996: 140.
147 Pl. *Phlb.* 48a–50b, esp.48d–e. On the influence of Plato's views of laughter on Aristotle see Fortenbaugh 2003b: 92.
148 See Baudelaire in Corrigan: 464.
149 For an analysis along similar lines but combining concepts of playful laughter and consequential laughter see Millett 2007: 32.
150 Frye in Corrigan: 147.
151 Duprey in Corrigan: 246.
152 See Habicht 1997: 123.
153 Arist. *Po.* 6 (1449b24–28). See mention of catharsis also in Arist. *Pol.* 8.7.1341b39–41.
154 Ar. *Po.* 5 1449a31–36, transl. Halliwell (Loeb).
155 Theophrastus appears to have accepted 'catharsis' as a concept, as is evident from his comments on the cathartic effect of music: see Apollonius, *Amazing Stories* 49.1–3 = fr. 726A. For discussion see Sicking 1998: 97–142 esp. 141.
156 See Janko 1984: 82–3, Cooper 1969: 65–71 and Golden 1987: 166.
157 See Fortenbaugh 2003b: 106.
158 Janko proposes that scorn and over-confidence are the emotions purged by comedy: see Janko 1984: 143. Other suggestions are anger and envy: see Cooper 1969: 66.
159 On indignation and comedy see Golden 1987: 169.
160 Meredith in Corrigan: 469.
161 Here Casanova is referring to Menander but the same may equally be said of Theophrastus. See Casanova 2013: 142.

162 On comedy and ethics as an effective combination generally see Meredith in Corrigan: 468 and Bergson in the same at 477. On Theophrastus' *Characters* in particular see Volt 2010: 319, Halliwell 2008: 237–8.

References

Anderson, W. 1970. *Theophrastus: The Character Sketches* (Kent, OH: Kent State University Press).

Barigazzi, A. 1965. *La formazione spirituale di Menandro* (Turin: Bottega d'Erasmo).

Baudelaire, C. [1855]. 'On the Essence of Laughter' reprinted in Corrigan 1965: 448–465.

Bergson, H. [1900]. 'Laughter' reprinted in Corrigan 1965: 471–477.

Boyce, B. 1967. *The Theophrastan Character in England to 1642* (London: Frank Cass & Co.).

Casanova, A. 2013. 'Menander and the Peripatos: New Insights into and Old Question'. In A. H. Sommerstein (ed.) *Menander in Contexts* (New York: Routledge): 137–151.

Cinaglia, V. 2013. 'Menander, Aristotle, Chance and Accidental Ignorance'. In A. H. Sommerstein (ed.) *Menander in Contexts* (New York: Routledge): 152–166.

Cooper, L. 1969. *An Aristotelian Theory of Comedy* (New York: Kraus Reprint Co.).

Corrigan, R. W. (ed.) 1965. *Comedy: Meaning and Form* (San Francisco: Chandler Publishing).

Csapo, E. 2010. 'The Production and Performance of Comedy in Antiquity'. In G. W. Dobrov (ed.) *Brill's Companion to the Study of Greek Comedy* (Leiden: Brill): 103–142.

Csapo, E. 2014. 'Performing Comedy in the Fifth through Early Third Centuries.' In M. Fontaine and A. C. Scafuro (eds) *The Oxford Handbook of Greek and Roman Comedy* (Oxford: Oxford University Press): 50–69.

De Temmerman, K. 2014. *Crafting Characters: Heroes and Heroines in the Ancient Greek Novel* (Oxford: Oxford University Press).

Diggle, J. 2004. *Theophrastus Characters*. Cambridge Classical Texts and Commentaries 43. (Cambridge: Cambridge University Press).

Fortenbaugh, W. W. 1974. 'Menander's *"Perikeiromene"*: Misfortune, Vehemence and Polemon', *Phoenix* 28.4: 430–443.

Fortenbaugh, W. W. 2003a. 'Theophrastus on Emotion' in TS: 71–90.

Fortenbaugh, W. W. 2003b. 'An Aristotelian and Theophrastean Analysis of Laughter' in TS: 91–106.

Fortenbaugh, W. W. 2003c. 'Theophrastus on Delivery' in TS: 253–271.

Fortenbaugh, W. W. 2003d. 'Theophrastus on Comic Character' in TS: 295–306.

Fortenbaugh, W. W. 2003e. 'Theophrastus, Source no. 709 FHS&G' in TS: 307–316.

Fortenbaugh, W. W. 2005. *Theophrastus of Eresus: Sources for His Life, Writings, Thought and Influence*. Commentary Volume 8: Sources on Rhetoric and Poetics (Texts 666–713). (Leiden: E.J. Brill).

Fortenbaugh, W. W. 2011. *Theophrastus of Eresus*. Commentary Volume 6.1. Sources on Ethics (Leiden: E.J. Brill).

Gaiser, K. 1967. 'Menander und der Peripatos', A & A 13: 8–40.

Goldberg, S. M. 1980. *The Making of Menander's Comedy* (London: Athlone Press).

Golden, L. 1987. 'Comic Pleasure', *Hermes* 115: 165–174.

Green, P. 1990. *Alexander to Actium: The Historical Evolution of the Hellenistic Age* (Berkeley and Los Angeles: University of California Press).

Habicht, C. 1997. *Athens from Alexander to Antony* (Cambridge, MA, and London: Harvard University Press).

Haegemans, K. 2001. 'Character Drawing in Menander's *Dyskolos*: Misanthropy and Philanthropy', *Mnemosyne* 54.6: 675–696.

Halliwell, S. 1995. Aristotle. *Poetics*. (Cambridge, MA, and London: Harvard University Press).

Halliwell, S. 2008. *Greek Laughter* (Cambridge: Cambridge University Press).

Hicks, E. L. 1882. 'On the Characters of Theophrastus', *JHS* 3: 128–143.

Hunter, R. L. 1985. *The New Comedy of Greece and Rome* (Cambridge: Cambridge University Press).

Hunter, R. L. 2014. 'Attic Comedy in the Rhetorical and Moralising Traditions'. In M. Revermann (ed.) *The Cambridge Companion to Greek Comedy* (Cambridge: Cambridge University Press): 373–386.

Ireland, S. 2010. 'New Comedy'. In G. W. Dobrov (ed.) *Brill's Companion to the Study of Greek Comedy* (Leiden: Brill): 333–396.

Janko, R. 1984. *Aristotle on Comedy: Towards a Reconstruction of Poetics II* (London: Duckworth).

Konstan, D. 2014. 'Crossing Conceptual Worlds: Greek Comedy and Philosophy'. In M. Fontaine and A. C. Scafuro (eds) *The Oxford Handbook of Greek and Roman Comedy* (Oxford: Oxford University Press): 278–294.

Lane Fox, R. 1996. 'Theophrastus' Characters and the Historian', *PCPhS* 42, 127–170.

Lape, S. and A. Moreno. 2014. 'Comedy and the Social Historian'. In M. Revermann (ed), *The Cambridge Companion to Greek Comedy* (Cambridge: Cambridge University Press): 336–369.

Lodge, D. 1992. *The Art of Fiction* (London: Secker and Warburg).

Lowe, N. J. 2001. 'Tragic Space and Comic Timing in Menander's *Dyskolos*' in Segal: 65–79.

Lowe, N. J. 2007. *Comedy: Greece & Rome*. New Surveys in the Classics No. 37 (Cambridge: Cambridge University Press).

Mc C. Brown, P.G. 1987. 'Masks, Names and Characters in New Comedy', *Hermes* 115: 181–202.

Meredith, G. [1877]. 'An Essay on Comedy' reprinted in Corrigan: 466–470.

Millett, P. 2007. *Theophrastus and His World*. Proceedings of the Cambridge Philological Society Supplementary Volume 33 (Cambridge: Cambridge University Press).

Nünlist, R. 2002. 'Speech within Speech in Menander'. In A. Willi (ed) *The Language of Greek Comedy* (Oxford: Oxford University Press): 219–260.

Pasquali, G. 1918. 'Sui "Caratteri" di Teofrasto', *RLC* 2: 73–79.

Perry, H.T.E. 1968. *Masters of Dramatic Comedy and their Social Themes* (New York: Kennikat Press).

Porter, M. 2005. *Windows of the Soul: Physiognomy in European Culture 1470–1780* (Oxford: Clarendon Press).

Roselli, D. K. 2011. *Theater of the People: Spectators and Society in Ancient Athens* (Austin: University of Texas Press).

Rosivach, V.J. 2000. 'The Audiences of New Comedy', *G&R* 47.2: 169–171.

Ruffell, I. 2014. 'Character Types'. In M. Revermann (ed) *The Cambridge Companion to Greek Comedy* (Cambridge: Cambridge University Press): 147–167.

Rusten, J. (ed.) 2011. *The Birth of Comedy: Texts, Documents, and Art from Athenian Comic Competitions, 486–280* (Baltimore: John Hopkins University Press).

Rusten, J. 2014. 'In Search of the Essence of Old Comedy: From Aristotle's Poetics to Zieliński, Cornford and Beyond'. In M. Fontaine and A. C. Scafuro (eds) *The Oxford Handbook of Greek and Roman Comedy* (Oxford: Oxford University Press): 33–49.

Rusten, J. and I. C. Cunningham. 2002. *Theophrastus Characters, Herodas Mimes, Sophron and Other Mime Fragments* (Cambridge, MA: Harvard University Press).

Scafuro, A. 2014a. 'Comedy in the Late Fourth and Early Third Centuries BCE'. In M. Fontaine and A. C. Scafuro (eds) *The Oxford Handbook of Greek and Roman Comedy* (Oxford: Oxford University Press): 199–217.

Scafuro, A.C. 2014b. 'Menander's Life and Oeuvre'. In M. Fontaine and A. C. Scafuro (eds) *The Oxford Handbook of Greek and Roman Comedy* (Oxford: Oxford University Press): 218–238.

Segal, E. (ed.) 2001. *Oxford Readings in Menander, Plautus and Terence* (Oxford: Oxford University Press).

Sicking, C. M. J. 1998. 'Theophrastus on the Nature of Music (716 FHS&G)'. In *RUSCH* Vol. VIII: 97–142.

Sollenberger, M.G. 2000. 'Diogenes Laertius' Life of Demetrius of Phalerum'. In *RUSCH* Vol. IX: 311–329.

Trenkner, S. 1958. *The Greek Novella in the Classical Period* (Cambridge: Cambridge University Press).

Ussher, R. G. 1977. 'Old Comedy and "Character": Some Comments', *G&R* 24: 71–79.

Vogt, S. 2006. 'Characters in Aristo'. In *RUSCH* Vol. XIII: 261–278.

Volt, Ivo. 2010. 'Not Valuing Others: Reflections of Social Cohesions in the *Characters* of Theophrastus'. In R. M. Rosen and I. Sluiter (eds) *Valuing Others in Classical Antiquity* (Leiden: Brill).

Wiles, D. 1991. *The Masks of Menander: Sign and Meaning in Greek and Roman Performances* (Cambridge: Cambridge University Press).

Willi, A. 2002. 'The Language of Greek Comedy: Introduction and Bibliographical Sketch'. In A. Willi (ed.), *The Language of Greek Comedy* (Oxford: Oxford University Press): 1–32.

4 Behaving badly
Ethics and the *Characters*

Theophrastus' character portraits are witty and entertaining illustrations of Athenian citizens behaving in inappropriate ways but, at the same time, they invite considered reflection on appropriate personal and social conduct. This topic falls squarely within the realm of ancient ethics.[1] There is, in fact, a discernible and meaningful ethical subtext underlying Theophrastus' carefully selected examples of behaviour.[2] Although there are some similarities between this subtext and Aristotle's ethical philosophy, Theophrastus' approach is uniquely different in important ways. Whereas Aristotle discusses ethical and unethical conduct in philosophical and abstract terms, Theophrastus offers a useful, realistic and practical illustration of the importance of ethical conduct. Theophrastus also demonstrates a particular interest in social dispositions, a subject in which he may have extended and clarified Aristotle's ethical theory.

Aristotle and Theophrastus on ethics and virtue

Aristotle's lectures on ethics, preserved in the *Nicomachean Ethics* and the *Eudemian Ethics*, have been widely studied.[3] Unfortunately, none of Theophrastus' works devoted to the subject of ethics have survived. Theophrastus' ethical teachings are known only from passages quoted in later sources.[4] These sources indicate that ethics was a major subject of enquiry for Theophrastus, as it was for Aristotle.[5] In the catalogue of Theophrastus' works recorded by Diogenes Laertius, at least thirty works on ethical topics are attributed to Theophrastus, including *Ethical Lectures*, *On Virtue*, *On Education*, *On Bringing up Children*, *On Happiness*, *On Good Fortune*, *On Kindness* and *On Flattery*.[6] The range of titles indicates that Theophrastus' interest in ethics overlapped with his interest in politics, religion, psychology, poetics and rhetoric, reflecting the interdisciplinary approach that was typical of the Peripatetic school overall (Chapter 1).[7]

Sources that quote Theophrastus' writings on ethics indicate that Theophrastus' views on ethics were similar to those of Aristotle.[8] For Aristotle, the study of ethics was primarily concerned with achieving *eudaimonia*, which is often translated as 'happiness' or 'thriving' but is perhaps better translated as 'good fortune'.[9] According to Aristotle, good fortune is achieved through virtuous action.[10] Similarly, Theophrastus viewed the fortunate and happy life as a virtuous and contemplative one.[11] For Aristotle, virtuous action requires practical intelligence that involves understanding virtue, recognising situations, and acting and responding appropriately.[12] Similarly, Theophrastus emphasised the importance of acquiring practical wisdom so that a person can judge how best to act in a situation.[13] To this end, Theophrastus particularly emphasised the importance of moral education for the young.[14] Like Aristotle, Theophrastus was also interested in various types and degrees of emotion and their effects.[15] Theophrastus was particularly critical of fault-finding and anger as well as extreme emotions such as envy and rage.[16]

Apart from a broad affinity in the views of Aristotle and Theophrastus on ethical subjects, there are also specific concurrences. In the *Nicomachean Ethics*, Aristotle defines virtue as a disposition that is engendered through practice and habit.[17] According to Aristotle, it is not enough to know what virtue is or to perform good actions in a mechanical way: one must know what one is doing and why, and choose virtuous action for its own sake.[18] The virtuous disposition involves (to use Aristotle's cumbersome phrasing) manifesting the right state, at the right time, about the right things, towards the right people, for the right end and in the right way.[19] This virtuous state is not a fixed standard but is relative to the individual and changes according to the circumstances.[20]

Theophrastus' definition of virtue as reported in later sources exactly mirrors Aristotle's definition in the *Nicomachean Ethics*. Theophrastus is reported to have said that "[virtue is] a disposition to choose, being in the mean which is relative to us, determined by reason and such as the practically wise man would determine it."[21] To illustrate this definition of virtue, Theophrastus gives an amusing example of appropriate behaviour based on a person's conduct at a meeting:

> Theophrastus says, during meetings one man goes through many things and chatters at length, another says little and not even what is essential, but a third says only what is necessary and so lays hold upon due measure. This is the mean relative to us, for it is determined by us by means of reason.[22]

Like Aristotle, Theophrastus emphasises that the 'virtuous mean' (sometimes called the golden mean) is not a fixed intermediate standard between two extremes but a standard that is relative to us and must be judged at the time and according to the circumstances.[23] Theophrastus' humorous and practical example of appropriate conduct at a meeting fits well with the style and tone of the *Characters*.

In defining the virtuous state, Aristotle identifies thirteen pairs of 'vices' along with a corresponding virtue.[24] So, for example, both recklessness and cowardice are to be avoided as inappropriate extremes while courage is the appropriately balanced, virtuous and 'mean' state that the ethical man should aspire to achieve.[25] Other examples of ethical triads described by Aristotle are lack of feeling, temperance and intemperance;[26] stinginess, generosity and profligacy;[27] and passivity, gentleness and irascibility.[28] Of the twenty-six vices analysed by Aristotle, nine overlap with negative character traits that feature in Theophrastus' *Characters*, namely, cowardice, obtuseness, stinginess, dissembling, boorishness, boastfulness, shamelessness, obsequiousness and flattery.[29]

In his lost ethical works, Theophrastus is said to have followed Aristotle's example and investigated a number of ethical triads, including: gentleness, irascibility and lack of feeling; courage, rashness and cowardice; and liberality, prodigality and meanness.[30] In discussing these virtues and vices, Theophrastus followed Aristotle's concept of the golden mean in holding that "some are bad on account of excess or deficiency in regard to emotions; others are good, obviously on account of being mean-dispositions."[31] Again, there is an overlap between what we know of these ethical studies and the traits that are personified in the *Characters*, especially Theophrastus' portraits of the *Coward*, the *Shabby Profiteer* and the *Arrogant Man*.

If we apply the model of ethical triads to the *Characters*, we can see that some of Theophrastus' character types can be paired up as opposing extremes relative to a particular virtue while others have no corresponding pair. Theophrastus' *Obsequious Man* and *Self-Centred Man*, for example, are two extremes relative to the virtue of friendliness.[32] The *Obsequious Man* praises his friends excessively, refuses to take sides in an arbitration and denigrates himself in order to please his host. *The Self-Centred Man* manifests the opposing defect: he is exceedingly unfriendly, dismissive and difficult. Other examples of 'excessive' types are the *Chatterbox*, who talks unendingly about trivial subject matter, and the *Superstitious Man* who is overly concerned to protect himself from divine disfavour. Examples of 'deficient' types are the *Coward*,[33] who fears even non-existent dangers, and the *Penny-Pincher* who refuses to lend even the most trifling of goods. In short, Theophrastus' choice of behavioural traits has some affinity with the behavioural traits analysed by Aristotle in his ethical works.

The uniqueness of Theophrastus' approach to ethics in the *Characters*

Although Theophrastus generally agrees with Aristotle's ethical philosophy and he examines similar traits to those examined by Aristotle, Theophrastus' descriptions of character types are also uniquely different in important ways. Firstly, Theophrastus deals only with vices.[34] This is in stark contrast to Aristotle's approach in the *Nicomachean Ethics* in which both virtues and vices are discussed. Secondly, Theophrastus uses humour to exaggerate the negative character traits, and he focusses on some vices that are absent from Aristotle's works.[35] Thirdly, Theophrastus does not analyse the behaviour that he describes.[36] Some scholars have interpreted these differences to mean that Theophrastus did not write the *Characters* for an ethical purpose[37] whereas, in fact, Theophrastus' work demonstrates a new and innovative approach to ethics and, in some respects, it may extend Aristotle's ethical theory.

Firstly, let us examine the differences between Theophrastus' and Aristotle's approach. Although it is true that Theophrastus focusses only on vices and does not portray any 'good' types in his *Characters*, the descriptions of negative behavioural traits nevertheless imply a virtuous mean. As Lane Fox has observed, 'good behaviour' can be inferred from the descriptions and it is situated exactly where

Aristotle would have located it: "to one side of the Characters' excesses".[38] It is obvious that certain forms of behaviour are inappropriate, such as the *Shabby Profiteer* who leaves town just to avoid sending a present for a friend's wedding (30.19–20), or the *Coward* who deliberately hides his sword to avoid fighting (25.4), or the *Arrogant Man* who hosts a dinner but refuses to dine with his guests (24.9). Conversely, it is not difficult to discern what the appropriate behaviour would be in the same circumstances.

Secondly, the emphasis on vices does not indicate a lack of interest or concern for 'good' qualities on Theophrastus' part. On the contrary, Theophrastus is keenly interested in ethical conduct and this is the driving motive behind the *Characters*. Theophrastus' definition of a comic jest (discussed in Chapter 3) means that, by definition, the 'rebuke' of inappropriate behaviour cannot rest on an *explicitly* stated principle of 'good' behaviour. Instead, it depends upon an implicit understanding of what 'good' behaviour entails. Thus, Theophrastus carefully selects only those forms of behaviour that would be widely regarded as inappropriate.

A further reason for Theophrastus' emphasis on vices is that the rules underlying social etiquette can be subtle and difficult to state in the positive, whereas breaches of those rules illustrate the virtuous ideal more clearly and effectively. There is, for example, no overt rule about having to make eye contact when passing people in the street. However, when Theophrastus' *Arrogant Man* consistently refuses to make any eye contact at all, deliberately averting his gaze, and only raising his head to look at people *when he feels like it* (24.8), this conduct is indicative of his disdain for others and his attitude of superiority. In his character portraits, Theophrastus carefully identifies precisely what makes the behaviour inappropriate, whether it is the manner in which it is done, inappropriate timing, poor choice of words, or an inappropriate expression or gesture, so that the breach of social etiquette is readily apparent.

The reason for Theophrastus' emphasis on some forms of vice over others is simply that Theophrastus only deals with forms of vice that are common.[39] Even Aristotle admitted that some vices do not have a name because persons of that type are uncommon.[40] Aristotle explicitly says that the rash man, for example, has no name and is not truly an excessive type because his boldness is mostly pretence.[41] Likewise, Theophrastus does not include a rash man, a profligate man or a type who has complete and utter disregard for the gods (the opposite of the *Superstitious Man*). Thus, Theophrastus' choices of subject reflect his eminently practical approach to ethics.[42]

A further reason for Theophrastus' emphasis on vice is that a series of character portraits of good and virtuous citizens going about their daily business would lack interest and appeal.[43] Vices, follies and inappropriate behaviour are far more interesting to observe.[44] As Millett notes, "collections of 'good' characters consistently fail to engage the reader, in that nothing about their behaviour can be provocative or piquant" while bad behaviour, so long as it is not truly evil, "would seem to be endlessly diverting".[45] Furthermore, if Pasquali is correct in his assertion that Theophrastus presented his character portraits as 'illustrative showpieces' for his lectures on ethics,[46] then Theophrastus' descriptions of character needed to be engaging. Theophrastus' entertaining and instructive descriptions of negative character types would have appealed to students within the Peripatos as well as to external audiences.[47]

Although Theophrastus' mode of presentation is markedly different from Aristotle's, there are good reasons for this difference. As Diggle has observed, "Aristotle provides the seed from which Theophrastus' descriptions grow."[48] Building upon Aristotle's abstract analysis of moral virtues and vices, Theophrastus takes Aristotle's ethical model and applies it to a practical, real-world study of Athenian citizens.[49] Rather than *telling* us why particular behaviour is inappropriate, Theophrastus simply *shows* us how the absence of that virtue manifests itself.[50] In doing so, Theophrastus provides a guide to recognising deficient moral qualities. This practical application of ethics to everyday life is unique and it represents a more effective method of ethical instruction than abstract philosophy.[51] While a positive description of a virtuous character provides a model of good behaviour, a portrait of negative behaviour is instructive, pointed and more memorable.

Theophrastus may also have extended Aristotle's ethical theory by clarifying the importance of ethical conduct in social contexts. In the *Nicomachean Ethics*, Aristotle recognises that social dispositions like friendliness, truthfulness and wittiness are virtues[52] but in the *Eudemian Ethics*, Aristotle contradicts this, saying that friendliness, truthfulness and wittiness are praiseworthy but are not virtues.[53] Fortenbaugh has suggested that Theophrastus' ethical treatises may have sought to resolve this disagreement in Aristotle's writings, by more clearly describing social dispositions like friendliness and discussing their relationship to emotion.[54] If this is the case, then perhaps the *Characters* was also part of Theophrastus' efforts to 'prove' the importance of certain social dispositions, by describing negative dispositions and illustrating their damaging effects on social life and interaction.

In sum, Theophrastus' *Characters* represents a new and innovative approach to the subject of ethics. Theophrastus answers the question of what constitutes ethical conduct by providing a series of negative examples, rather than repeating Aristotle's abstract analysis of how best to behave. This approach is highly practical and memorable. To this end, the tone is much lighter than Aristotle's ethical works and the presentation is simple and economical so as not to detract from the liveliness of the subject. The ethical lesson is more engaging because it is presented in a comic framework.[55] Furthermore, the act of laughing at these various types of men behaving badly engenders a shared sense of reprobation that is, in itself, a highly effective method of teaching and reinforcing social ethics.

In search of the Theophrastean ideal

Some commentators have inferred that behind Theophrastus' *Characters* there lies a Theophrastean 'ideal citizen'. Boyce, for example, says that the *Characters* implies that a "normal, admirable character is possible" but he does not venture to describe such a character.[56] Millett goes further, saying that the work demonstrates "how to be good at being a citizen in the context of a democratic polis".[57] Compared to Aristotle's 'Great-Hearted Man', Millett maintains that Theophrastus' guide to conduct is eminently more realistic, contextualised and grounded.[58] Millett labels this ideal the 'Theophrastus Man': "the Peripatetic ideal of a citizen, tempered to suit the circumstances of a democratically-minded polis".[59] But what does this ideal 'Theophrastus Man' look like and how does he behave? And how can we ensure that we faithfully interpret Theophrastus' ideal without imposing modern values and expectations about behaviour and social etiquette?[60]

We need to be cautious about inverting the character descriptions and trying to read them as a positive set of rules of conduct. If we invert Theophrastus' exaggerated pictures of behaviour,[61] a similarly distorted picture will result. The behaviour of the *Superstitious Man*, for example, is deliberately exaggerated and cannot simply be inverted in order to attain a reliable picture of proper religious practice.[62] At other times, the inappropriateness of the conduct is heavily dependent on context and does not imply a fixed rule for all circumstances. The *Tactless Man*, for example, asks for advice when a companion is busy, and suggests a walk when his companions are exhausted after a long journey (12.2,7). There is no issue *per se* with the conduct: asking for advice or suggesting a walk are reasonable activities. It is all a question of timing, degree and good judgement.

These challenges have not deterred historians from inferring a great deal about ancient Athenian life from the *Characters*. Millett, for example, relies on the work as evidence for lending and borrowing practices.[63] More recently, he has used the *Characters* to examine key aspects of Athenian social life, including notions of honour, interaction with slaves, relations with women, education, hospitality, social interaction, greetings, conversation, reciprocity and exchange.[64] Lane Fox extracts information about Attic objects and practices, subscriptions and arbitrations, lending and borrowing, eating and dining, married love and children.[65] Volt examines conduct in the Assembly, the law courts, the theatre and religious behaviour.[66] It would seem then that the *Characters* can be a useful and fruitful source of information if read in a careful and considered way.

One possibility that has not been fully explored is reading the *Characters* as a guide to how citizens should behave, particularly with respect to widespread values such as shame, disgrace and friendship.[67] Millett has observed that:

> Theophrastus has created for his audience an implied code of conduct: a perspective on honour and shame, co-operation and conflict, as they might impinge on upper class citizens with reference to the civic society peculiar to democratic Athens.[68]

Taking this suggestion further, we will examine the possibility of reading the *Characters* as a commentary on three important social dispositions: friendship, love of humanity and shame.

Case study 1: friendship[69]

In ancient Greek texts, the most common term used to denote a 'friend' is the noun *philos*.[70] Friendship was, as Konstan argues, a sign of civic solidarity among 'good citizens' in ancient Athens.[71] It involved an intimate and close connection,[72] with expectations to assist[73] and an expectation of help in return.[74] Conduct that contravenes these expectations of friendship is one of the most important topics in the *Characters*.[75] Although a variety of different relationships feature in the sketches, including patron and client, host and guest, foreign friends and dinner companions, the discussion that follows will focus on persons explicitly described by Theophrastus in the sketches as 'friends' or *philoi*.[76]

The centrality of the theme of friendship in the *Characters* echoes a broader interest that Theophrastus had in the topic of friendship. Diogenes Laertius records that Theophrastus wrote a work on the subject in three books.[77] In his will, Theophrastus urged his followers to hold the property of the school in common as 'friends' in a spirit of unity and philosophical purpose.[78] Extracts of Theophrastus' writings in later sources indicate that Theophrastus had firm notions about an ideal of friendship but tempered this ideal with a realistic perspective.[79] Thus, while Theophrastus is said to have recognised the special nature of true friendship, placing it above all other forms of affection, he also commented on its rarity in human affairs.[80] This juxtaposition of philosophical ideal and harsh reality is reflected in the *Characters*, where a virtuous ideal of friendship is glimpsed through Theophrastus' descriptions of character types treating friends poorly.

The first theme that emerges from Theophrastus' depictions of friends in the *Characters* is that only certain categories of individuals should potentially be one's friends. Enemies should not be treated as friends, whereas the *Dissembler* deliberately seeks out his enemies to chat with them (1.2).[81] This goes against the grain of popular morality, which regarded kindness as a mark of friendship and enmity as part and parcel of life.[82] Slaves should not be regarded as friends either: the *Country Bumpkin* treats his slaves and hired labourers as friends, rather than employees, by discussing important business matters with them (4.3).[83] Criminal types and morally degraded people should also be avoided. In the sketch of the *Friend of Villains*, for example, the term 'villain' encompasses not only wicked people but also those standing trial and those who have been defeated in the law courts (29.2, 6).[84]

Once a friendship has been established, it is appropriate to show a genuine interest in, and concern for, one's friends.[85] The *Rumour-Monger* engages in "empty courtesies"[86] with a friend pretending to inquire after his health and his news. Before his friend can answer, he interrupts and begins sharing his own fabricated stories (8.2). On the battlefield, the *Coward* pretends to be genuinely concerned about his injured friend when, in fact, he uses his friend's injury as a pretext not to enter the battlefield (25.5). At a dinner party for his friends, the *Arrogant Man* does not eat with his friends but tells one of his employees to look after them (24.9). In doing this, he contravenes the expected guest-host relationship and shows disregard for his friends.[87] When the *Obtuse Man* receives a message notifying him of a friend's death and inviting him to the funeral, his physical response is appropriate (he bursts into tears), but his words are not, since he says, "And the best of luck to him" (14.7).[88]

Honesty, trust and gratitude emerge as important and closely interrelated aspects of friendship.[89] When the *Shabby Profiteer* has wine for sale, for example, he sells it to a friend watered down (30.5). This conduct not only involves a dishonest transaction but takes advantage of the friend's trust. The *Country Bumpkin* does not trust his friends and family, as would be expected, but instead trusts his employees (4.3). Gratitude for genuinely kind acts performed by a friend is also expected.[90] The *Ungrateful Grumbler*, for example, is brought a parcel of food sent by a friend but he complains that he was cheated out of the soup and wine by not being invited to dinner (17.2). This response demonstrates ingratitude as well as the attribution of dishonest motives to the friend.

How one speaks about one's friends to others is presented as a clear indicator of one's real attitude towards them. It is inappropriate to slander one's friends to others, or conversely, to defend bad people as if they are friends. The *Slanderer* especially likes to speak ill of his own friends, claiming that it is not slander but an exercise of free speech (28.6).[91] The *Disagreeable Man* describes his friends as a "leaking jar" and unable to be gratified by kindnesses (20.9). In doing so, the *Disagreeable Man* presents himself as a beneficent friend and generous host, but he also damages the reputation of his friends by portraying them as insatiable and perhaps also wasteful.[92] Conversely, one should not defend villains and portray them as friends. Theophrastus' *Friend of Villains* defends wicked people, saying that they have been mislabelled and misunderstood (29.4–5).

Willingness to help out financially can be a real test of friendship. In ancient Athens, a subscription was a sum of money lent by friends and acquaintances to help out during hard times and expected to be paid back at a later date.[93] Theophrastus deals with various aspects of the subscription process in the *Characters* and, in so doing, he reveals the norms of conduct that surrounded this activity. If the *Illiberal Man* hears that a friend is collecting money, for example, he will deliberately avoid him by cutting down a side-street and taking a circuitous route home (22.9). If a friend asks the *Self-Centred Man* for a contribution to a subscription, he will refuse at first, but reluctantly pay at a later time saying that it is "more money wasted" (15.7). The *Dissembler*, on the other hand, pretends not to have any money (1.5).[94] The *Boastful Man* vastly exaggerates the sums he has given out as loans to friends (23.6). When friends collect a subscription for the *Ungrateful Grumbler* in an effort to cheer him up, he asks how he can possibly be happy when he has to refund each contribution *and* be grateful for the favour (17.9).

In summary, the *Characters* implies that good friendships are possible, if they are based on a genuine concern for one another, honesty, trust, gratitude, kind words, and a willingness to help and be helped. A similar concern with helpfulness, kind words, fidelity and longevity emerges from a collection of sayings attributed to Theophrastus on the subject of friendship:[95]

> Friendships ought to be immortal. A man without friends is worth as much as a body without soul. Conversations with friends ought to be brief, friendships long. . . . Be at the service of a fortunate friend when invited, an unfortunate

one even if not invited. . . . It is right for you to grant those things to a friend which you would wish to be granted to you. The fidelity of a friend is the bond of friendship.[96]

In an ideal world, friendship is highly valuable and companionship, help and generosity are key to forming and maintaining friendships. At the same time, Theophrastus' *Characters* is eminently realistic in recognising the potential for friendships to turn sour. This also reflects Theophrastus' views in the ancient sources, when he advises that one should carefully test and evaluate a friend before entering into friendship with them.[97] He warns against friends that are constant flatterers[98] and he comments on how friendship can bear ignorance and mistakes but cannot bear envy and ill-will.[99] As in the *Characters*, Theophrastus is concerned for the way in which friends are spoken of, with Theophrastus advising that a friend should never be hurt, not even with a joke[100] since hurt friends will show their anger.[101]

Once a friendship is firmly established, there is great scope for generosity, helpfulness and sharing. Theophrastus is said to have commented that it is appropriate to assist a friend who is suffering a misfortune without waiting to be called upon.[102] He also held the view that the possessions and friends of friends should be held in common[103] and that there are even times when assisting a friend will be more important than strictly adhering to the law.[104] This is a more extreme view than Aristotle's and, according to Konstan, Theophrastus may have been trying to fill a gap in Aristotle's exposition on this topic.[105]

Theophrastus clearly perceived friendship as worthwhile and important for one's well-being[106] and this is consistent with views on friendship from the ancient Greek world generally.[107] Like Aristotle's analysis of friendship in the *Nicomachean Ethics*, Theophrastus distinguished between three kinds of friendship: the first based on virtue, and two others based on pleasure and utility.[108] Theophrastus held that the friendship based on virtue is the rarest and therefore the most valuable[109] but his cautious and common sense approach also reflects the "essentially prudential nature of Greek theory about friendship".[110] One area in which Theophrastus may differ from earlier Greek writers is his emphasis on absolute honesty and candour between friends.[111] These values are said to be "prominent in discussions of friendship only in the Hellenistic and Roman periods".[112]

Case study 2: love of humanity

In the fourth century, the term *philanthropia* (literally, "love of humanity") was widely used to denote a person who by his speech and actions showed himself to be friendly and kind to his fellow men.[113] It could involve personal relationships between citizens as well as wider relationships between neighbours, assemblies and allies.[114] In Theophrastus' *Characters*, there are many examples of forms of behaviour that contravene important socio-ethical norms,[115] but there are three character types in particular who demonstrate a failure to be kind to their fellows: the *Arrogant Man*, the *Self-Centred Man* and the *Ungrateful Grumbler*.

Each of these portraits portrays a different aspect of the vice of unsociability and unkindness.[116]

The *Arrogant Man* thinks that he is superior to his fellows and this attitude has a negative impact on all his dealings with others, including visitors, friends and fellow citizens. He ignores the unwritten rules of personable meetings and greetings.[117] He is never the one to make the first approach and avoids eye contact with others (24.7–9). He reminds other people of the favours he has done for them (3) and, when he travels, he sends someone ahead to announce his arrival (10). In transactions, he treats others disdainfully or deliberately inconveniences them (7). He is self-important, claiming that he cannot accept an important office because he simply has 'no time'.[118] In short, he "thinks only of his own convenience, and treats others high-handedly or ignores them".[119]

Unlike the *Arrogant Man*, the *Self-Centred Man* does not believe that he is superior but is generally unsociable, uncooperative and surly. He does not bother to return a greeting, he does not wait long for anyone; and if asked where someone is, he says "Don't bother me" (15.3, 4, 9). He is bad-tempered and does not forgive others readily, even if they bump into him by accident (6). In transactions, he is self-centred and unhelpful: when he has something for sale, he refuses to tell customers how much he will sell it for but, instead, asks *them* what he can get for it (4). As Diggle observes, this refusal to name a price contravenes the unwritten rules of bargaining and haggling.[120] The *Self-Centred Man* even refuses to give appropriate offerings to the gods (11).

The *Ungrateful Grumbler* suffers from a very specific form of misanthropy: he is never satisfied with his lot and is incapable of recognising good fortune. When a lady-friend is kissing him, he says to her, "I wonder if your affection really comes from the heart?" (17.3). When he finds a purse in the street, he complains that he has never found a treasure (5). When a person brings him the good news that he has a son, he says, "If you add 'And you have lost half your fortune' you will not be far wrong" (7). The *Ungrateful Grumbler* introduces a sour note into all of his relationships because he always suspects that he is getting less than he is entitled to. He is also unable to accept kindnesses because he resents the expectation to repay the favour.[121]

Acts of generosity and hospitality were regarded as important demonstrations of *philanthropia*.[122] Two character portraits particularly illustrate the failure to provide appropriate hospitality. Firstly, there is the *Penny-Pincher*, who is obsessed with holding onto his property. He counts the number of cups each guest drinks, he provides small servings of food and makes the smallest offering to the gods (10.3, 12). Secondly, there is the *Shabby Profiteer*, who is determined to extract some benefit from acting as host however small that benefit might be. He claims that he is entitled to a double helping because he is serving out the food (30.4). He makes an inventory of the leftovers (16) and he charges his guests for various sundry expenses (18).

In a similar vein, there are many references in Theophrastus' *Characters* to the practice of borrowing items from friends or neighbours. Lending and borrowing household items was commonplace in ancient Athens[123] and it was a mark of kindness, reciprocity, and community spirit.[124] Yet, there is also an etiquette to be observed when borrowing an item to which the *Shameless Man* pays no heed. He goes to a neighbour's house to borrow consumable products such as barley or straw and treats his neighbour like a slave by making him deliver the goods to his doorstep (9.7).[125] The *Shabby Profiteer* borrows money from a visitor who is staying with him presumably because the visitor will be unlikely to demand repayment once he has left town (30.3). He borrows from other delegates when he is abroad on public service duties, leaving his own official travel allowance at home (7), and he borrows a cloak from a friend and does not return it until his friend demands it back (10).

For lenders too, there is an etiquette to be followed. A lender should not be overly anxious about the items he has lent, unlike the *Country Bumpkin* who lies awake in the middle of the night thinking about his plough, basket, sickle and sack (4.11). The *Penny-Pincher* is an even more extreme case and forbids his wife from lending even the cheapest and most inconsequential of items such as salt, a lamp-wick or herbs (10.13). The *Distrustful Man* will only lend items to individuals who can be trusted (such as his family members) and, if he must lend items, he makes a point of carefully checking the items and securing a guarantee about the cost of replacement (18.7).

Theophrastus' character portraits demonstrate that an attitude of kindness, hospitality and generosity is important for good relations between men, and this is a view expressed by Theophrastus elsewhere in other sources.[126] Theophrastus agreed with Aristotle that it is humanity that binds people together and that people are by nature well-disposed towards each other.[127] Theophrastus is reported to have said: "all men [are related] to each other, for one of two reasons: either because they have the same ancestors or because they share food and customs and the same race."[128] According to Theophrastus, two positive attributes that bind men together are kindness and honour.[129] Kindness is both noble and advantageous and, according to Theophrastus, doing a favour or kindness should not be regretted, especially since it can "bear noble fruit".[130] Elsewhere, Theophrastus says that one ought to remember by whom one has been well treated (rather than ill-treated) because expressing thanks is a mark of good character.[131]

Case study 3: shame

Shame can be defined as a "kind of pain or uneasiness in respect of misdeeds, past, present, or future, which seem to tend to bring dishonour".[132] Shame was an important concept in ancient Greek culture.[133] As Fortenbaugh observes: "[f]or the most part it was regarded in a positive light, but it could be viewed negatively as an undesirable character trait that manifests itself in hesitation and inactivity."[134] On the subject of shame, Theophrastus offers highly practical advice.[135] For Theophrastus, shame is a positive attribute since it shows an awareness of a lack of virtue and the ability to distinguish right from wrong.[136] If one has a solid awareness of right and wrong, one will feel ashamed of doing wrong and avoid making a mistake in the first place.[137] If wrongdoing occurs and the doer feels intense shame, this will show through physical signs such as blushing red, which is taken as a positive sign that the agent is conscious of his/her wrongdoing.[138] Theophrastus allegedly saw a youth blush and said: "Cheer up! For virtue has just such a colour."[139] For Theophrastus, shame and self-respect go hand in hand. Theophrastus is recorded as saying: "Have respect for yourself and you will not feel shame before someone else."[140]

Theophrastus' *Shameless Man* is an interesting and complex type. He knows how he ought to behave but disregards social proprieties in the interest of pursuing benefits or savings for himself. When his overseas guests are going to the theatre, for example, he joins them at the performance but does not pay for his own seat or offer to pay for theirs (9.5). The following day, he uses the same tickets again for his sons and their slave (5–6). When he has held a sacrifice, instead of hosting a feast as would be expected, he preserves the meat and dines at someone else's house, feeding his slave first without asking the host (3).[141]

The *Repulsive Man* is also shameless, in this case, about matters of appearance, propriety and modesty:

> The Repulsive Man is the kind who lifts up his clothes and exposes himself in front of ladies. At the theatre he applauds when no one else is applauding and hisses actors whose performance the audience is enjoying, and when silence has fallen he raises his head and burps to make spectators turn round. When the market is at its busiest he goes to the shops which sell nuts, myrtle-berries or fruit, and stands munching away while chatting idly to the shopkeeper. . . . And he stops in front of the hairdresser's or the perfumer's and explains that he intends to get drunk.
>
> (11.2–9)

The *Repulsive Man*'s conduct in the presence of freeborn women is indecent;[142] and while a lively theatre audience was the norm, the inappropriate timing of the *Repulsive Man*'s conduct makes it particularly disruptive and distracting. As for his conduct in the marketplace, he disgraces himself by frequenting disreputable venues.[143]

The *Slanderer* too is shameless, in his vicious commentary about his fellows. When asked to share what he knows about a certain individual, he says that the man changed his name to disguise the fact that he is a runaway slave and that he is a "criminal with a tattoo" (28.2). He continues his slanderous speech by categorising certain houses as brothels and denigrating the women who live in them (3–4). When he hears others slandering a person, he joins in enthusiastically and adds, "There's nobody I detest more than that man. He's got a repulsive face. And his depravity has no equal" (4). His shameless slander reaches a climax with abuse of his own friends and relatives as well as the dead (6).[144]

In the *Characters*, Theophrastus illustrates that the capacity to feel shame is an important indicator of virtue. Individuals who behave shamelessly are either unwilling to distinguish, or incapable of distinguishing, right from wrong in the relevant circumstances.[145] Conversely, modesty, propriety, good timing and social etiquette are important indicators that an individual has an appropriate under-standing of virtuous conduct and can apply this understanding to social situations. Shame moderates behaviour in social settings. It encourages individuals to be self-aware and it ensures that dealings between people are conducted with pro-priety and respectability.[146] In the *Characters*, Theophrastus gives a practical and useful demonstration of the negative effects of an absence of shame.

Conclusion

The *Characters* represents an innovative approach to the subject of ethics. By presenting humorous, lively and realistic portraits of a range of types who behave badly, Theophrastus solidly grounds Aristotle's theory of moral virtue in real life contexts. In doing so, Theophrastus expands upon the ethical theory of Aristo-tle to demonstrate that social ethics are important[147] both for their own sake and as expressions of personal virtues. The *Characters* demonstrates that negative character traits can have a serious impact on social relationships and can damage societal norms and expectations. In particular, the work demonstrates that friend-ship, love of humanity and shame are important social virtues that help to regulate conduct and to smooth the pathways of social interaction.

The emphasis on friendliness, shame and love of humanity no doubt gives some insight into the values and attributes that Theophrastus himself admired. Certainly, the sources on Theophrastus' life indicate that he took care with his friends, his work, his conduct and his appearance.[148] There is no excuse, in Theophrastus' world, for the sort of conduct engaged in by the *Shameless* or *Repulsive Man*, the *Ungrateful Grumbler* or the *Shabby Profiteer*. At the same time, the behaviours that are targeted by Theophrastus are also indicative of broader social values since character types, in order to be both successful and understood, presuppose a shared understanding and appreciation of certain moral values in society.[149] Thus there is a direct correlation between the values that Theophrastus points to in the *Characters* and the values that were widely admired by Athenians in the fourth century. In this way, the *Characters* can be a valuable source of information for the study of ethics in fourth-century Athe-nian society.

Notes

1 Scholars who regard the Characters as having an ethical orientation include Petersen 1859: 56–118, Navarre 1924: intro., Regenbogen 1940: 1500–11, Steinmetz 1959, Fortenbaugh 2011: 138. For arguments against an ethical purpose see Ussher 1960: 3–4, Diggle 2004: 12, Jebb-Sandys 10–17 and Furley 1953.
2 It is this ethical subtext that was capitalised upon by later authors such as Joseph Hall and La Bruyère seeking to demonstrate the "practical side of moral philosophy": see Millett 2007: 12.
3 The *Magna Moralia* is sometimes attributed to Aristotle but it is probably from a later period: see Crisp and Saunders 1999: 109. For a useful overview of Aristotle's *Nico-machean Ethics* see Miller 2011 and on Aristotle's ethics generally see Hughes 2001, and Crisp and Saunders 1999: at 141–3.

4 See frs. 436–579B, analysed in Fortenbaugh 2011. For a useful bibliography on Theophrastean ethics see Fortenbaugh 2011: 751–67.

5 See Ierodiakonou 2016.

6 See fr. 436 nos. 1–33, discussed in Fortenbaugh 2011: 121–30.

7 See Fortenbaugh 2011: 739.

8 Especially the views expressed by Aristotle in the *Eudemian Ethics*. See Fortenbaugh 2003b: 131.

9 See MacIntyre 1998: 39.

10 *EN* 10.7.1–2 (1177a12–18).

11 Ambrose, *On the Duties of Ministers* 2.2 = fr. 480B, and Cicero, *To Atticus* 2.16.3 = fr. 481.

12 *EN* 6.12.6–8 (1144a6–23). See discussion in Fortenbaugh 1969. Also MacIntyre 1998: 38.

13 Stobaeus, *Anthology* 3.19.12 = fr. 526.

14 Stobaeus, *Anthology* 2.31.124 = fr. 465.

15 See Fortenbaugh 2003a.

16 See frs 438, 443, 444, 446, 447 and 526. Discussed in Fortenbaugh 2003a.

17 *EN* 2.1.1–2 (1103a14–18).

18 *EN* 2.4.4–6 (1105b5–18).

19 *EN* 2.6.11–12 (1106b21–23).

20 *EN* 2.9.7–9 (1109b13–27). For a discussion of the significance of the particular situation see Fortenbaugh 1993.

21 Stobaeus, *Anthology* 2.7.20 = fr. 449A at 140. 5–6. Compare *EN* 2.6.15 (1107a1–3).

22 Stobaeus, *Anthology* 2.7.20 = fr.449A at 140.1–4.

23 Theophrastus says that the temperate man has an appetite for the right things at the right time and to the proper extent: Stobaeus, *Anthology* 2.7.20 = fr.449A at 141.14–19.

24 *EN* 2.7. 1–16 (1107b1–1108b10).

25 *EN* 2.7.2–3 (1107b1–4).

26 *EN* 3.10.1–3.12.10 (1117b23–1119b19).

27 *EN* 4.1.1–5 (1119b22–1120a3).

28 *EN* 4.5.1–14 (1125b25–1126b10).

29 See Diggle 2004: 6–7.

30 Stobaeus, *Anthology* 2.7.20 = fr.449A at 140.7–12, see Fortenbaugh 2011: 308–11 for a discussion of this list of coordinates.

31 Stobaeus, *Anthology* 2.7.20 = fr.449A at 141.13–14.

32 Aristotle discusses the same trio in *EN* 2.7.13–14 (1108a26–30). See Diggle 2004: 222.

33 Theophrastus' *Coward* can be viewed as a practical illustration of the topics Aristotle covers in his discussion of courage and cowardice (such as confronting death and facing a storm at sea): see *EN* 2.6.10–12 (1115a33–1115b6).

34 Rusten and Cunningham 2002: 20.

35 Jebb-Sandys: 11–13.

36 Rusten and Cunningham 2002: 20. It is for this reason that Fortenbaugh describes Theophrastus as dealing with 'superficial behavioural patterns'. Although I have not adopted Fortenbaugh's terminology, I agree with his analysis. See Fortenbaugh 2003b: 131–2, 141.

37 See Jebb-Sandys: 16–17 and Furley 1953: 59.

38 Lane Fox 1996: 140.

39 See Jebb-Sandys: 11–12.

40 *EN* 2.7.11 (1108a17–20).

41 *EN* 2.7.2 (1107b1–2).

42 On the practical reasons for portraying only negative types see Smeed 1985: 190–8.

43 Millett regards Aristotle's boring portrait of the 'Great-Hearted Man' as a "case in point" – see Millett 2007: 29.

44 On our psychological resistance to 'good' types see Smeed 1985: 192ff.
45 Millett 2007: 29. According to Boyce, "frail and wicked men are always more interesting": see Boyce 1967: 4.
46 See Diggle 2004: 15.
47 See Fortenbaugh 2011: 740, also Glucker 1998: 300 esp. n.4.
48 Diggle 2004: 7.
49 Diggle 2004: 7.
50 This reflects real life in that we observe good and bad manners but "do not investigate their motives": Fortenbaugh 2003b: 141.
51 Baltussen 2016: 88.
52 *EN* 4.6.1–4.8.12 (1126b11–1128b9 esp. at 1128b5–9).
53 *EE* 3.7.10 (1234a24–25).
54 Fortenbaugh 2011: 229.
55 On the combination of ethics and comedy see Diggle 2004: 9, Halliwell 2008: 237–8 and Lane Fox 1996: 141.
56 Boyce 1967: 13.
57 Millett 2007: 109.
58 Millett 2007: 29. For discussion see MacIntyre 1998: 51.
59 Millett 2007: 52.
60 See Millett 2007: 40–1.
61 Millett 2007: 39ff; Lane Fox 1996: 143, 154.
62 Lane Fox 1996: 152–4.
63 See Millett 1991.
64 See Millett (2007) on honour (70ff), interaction with slaves (74–7), relations with women (78–9), education (79), guests and dining (80–2), behaviour on the streets (83–5), greetings (85), conversation (85–92), reciprocity and exchange (93–8).
65 See Lane Fox 1996 for comments on objects and practices (143–5), subscriptions and arbitrations (146), lending and borrowing (147), eating and dining (148), and married love and children (148).
66 See Volt (2010) on the Assembly (306–8), law courts (308–9), theatre (310) and religion (311).
67 Lane Fox 1996: 154.
68 Millett 2007: 105.
69 On translating *philia* as friendship see Konstan 1997: 9, 67–72. Also see Millett 1991: 109ff.
70 Konstan argues that the concrete noun refers to those joined by a "voluntary bond of affection and good will" and that this group "normally excludes both close kin and more distant acquaintances, whether neighbors or fellow-citizens": Konstan 1997: 53. Theophrastus uses the term to refer to the bond between husbands and wives and also fathers and sons: see Aspasius, *On Aristotle's* Nicomachean Ethics 8.8 1158b11–28 = fr. 533.
71 Konstan 2010: 241.
72 Konstan 1997: 92.
73 Konstan 1997: 56–9.
74 Konstan 1997: 80. Also Ferguson 1958: 74.
75 Volt 2010: 312.
76 For a full list of the many references to *philia* in the *Characters* see Volt 2010: 312 n.47.
77 DL 5.45.165 = 436 no. 23a.
78 DL 5.52.312. See also Sollenberger 1992: 3811.
79 Jerome, *On Micah* 2.7 = fr. 532, and Seneca, *To Lucilius* 1.3.2 = 538B.
80 Jerome, *On Micah* 2.7 = fr. 532, discussion in Fortenbaugh 2011: 582.
81 On the deliberateness of the encounter, see Diggle 2004: 169.
82 Dover 1974: 181.

83 On slaves see Millett 2007: 73–7.
84 See Diggle 2004: 499.
85 *EN* 8.3.6 (1156b7–18).
86 Diggle 2004: 277.
87 See Millett 2007: 81.
88 See Diggle 2004: 337.
89 See Theophrastus' sayings on friendship compiled by Walter Burley, *On the Life and Character of Philosophers* 68, sayings 6–7, 10–11 = fr. 546. On generosity see Thomas of Ireland, *Flowers of Almost All Learned Men*, chap. On Friendship = fr. 536.
90 Volt 2010: 312ff.
91 See Diggle 2004: 498.
92 See Millett 2007: 96 and Diggle 2004: 402.
93 See Millett 1989: 41–3; Millett 2007: 96 and Volt 2010: 313. Although they were interest-free loans, they were expected to be repaid: see Lane Fox 1996: 146.
94 On some problems with this section of text see Diggle 2004: 175.
95 On the authenticity of these sayings see Fortenbaugh 2011: 628.
96 Walter Burley, *On the Life and Character of Philosophers* 68, sayings 2–12 = fr. 546.
97 Codex Vaticanus Graecus 1144 f. 210 v.20–1 = 538 A; also frs. 538B–F.
98 On flatterers as friends see Walter Burley, *On the Life and Character of Philosophers* 68, sayings 7–8 = fr. 546. Also Millett 1989 at 31–2.
99 Codex Vaticanus Graecus 1144 f.210 v.19–20 = fr. 540.
100 Walter Burley, *On the Life and Character of Philosophers* 68, saying 9–10 = fr. 546.
101 Walter Burley, *On the Life and Character of Philosophers* 68, sayings 8–9 = fr. 546.
102 Walter Burley, *On the Life and Character of Philosophers* 68, saying 6–7 = fr. 546.
103 Plutarch, *On Brotherly Love* 20 490E = fr. 535, also see frs 536–537.
104 See Gellius, *Attic Nights* 13–14 = fr. 534. For analysis see Fortenbaugh 1990.
105 Konstan suggests that the political climate in Athens may have influenced Theophrastus' views as this was a time when friendship with powerful political figures raised questions of an ethical nature: see Konstan 1997: 133. Theophrastus' relationship with Demetrius of Phalerum certainly represents an interesting case study. For a different view see Fortenbaugh (1990).
106 Fortenbaugh 2011: 745.
107 See Konstan 1997: 14–23. For Aristophanes' and Menander's praise of friendship see Ferguson 1958: 58. Also Isocrates' advice to Demonicus on friendship at 1.24–26.
108 *EN* 8.3.1 (1156a6–13); Aspasius, *On Aristotle's* Nicomachean Ethics 8.8 1158b11–28 = fr. 533, discussed in Fortenbaugh 1975: 52–4.
109 See Fortenbaugh 2011: 581–2.
110 Ferguson 1958: 59.
111 According to Theophrastus, "when the characters of friends are faultless, then community in all things, plans, desires should exist among them without any exception": Gellius, *Attic Nights* 1.3.13 = fr 534.
112 Konstan 1997: 15.
113 On uses of the term see Dover 1974: 201–2. Also Ferguson 1958: 107–9.
114 Ferguson 1958: 108.
115 See Halliwell 2008: 238, also Millett 2007: 95–6.
116 On kindness see Fortenbaugh 2011: 505–7.
117 See Millett 2007: 85.
118 For reasonable excuses for declining an office see Diggle 2004: 447.
119 Diggle 2004: 445.
120 Diggle 2004: 345.
121 See Diggle 2004: 376.
122 On hospitality, see Millett 2007: 81.

123 See Millett 1991: 37–9.

124 See Millett 2007: 95.

125 Millett 2007: 97.

126 Walter Burley, *On the Life and Character of Philosophers* 68, saying 10–11 = fr. 546. Theophrastus also wrote a work *On Kindness*, see DL 5.48 = fr. 1 = 436 no.24.

127 *EN* 8.1.3 (1155a20–23).

128 See Porphyry, *On Abstinence from Eating Animals* 3.25.1–4 = fr. 531; discussion in Fortenbaugh 2011: 550–570. Theophrastus' identification of a natural relationship between humans was further extended to man's relationship with animals (see frs. 531 and 584A). For discussion see Fortenbaugh 1971.

129 Stobaeus, *Anthology* 4.1.72 = fr. 517.

130 Pseudo-Aristotle, *Letters* 4.1–5 = fr. 518.

131 *Gnomologium Vaticanum*, no. 328 = fr. 525.

132 *Rh.* 2.6.2 (1383b) transl. Freese (Loeb). See also Williams 1993: 78.

133 See Dover 1974: 236–42, Williams 1993: 78ff, Millett 2007: 62.

134 Fortenbaugh 2011: 371.

135 Compare *EN* 4.9.3–8 (1128b19–36). Aristotle's brief account of shame in the *Rhetoric* simply concludes that men feel shame before individuals they respect: *Rh.* 2.6.25 (1385a).

136 See Fortenbaugh 2011: 299.

137 *Gnomologium Vaticanum*, no. 329 = fr. 473 and *Gnomologium Vaticanum*, no. 327 = 453; discussed by Fortenbaugh 2011: 375.

138 See *EN* 4.9.2 (1128b13); Fortenbaugh 2011: 372.

139 Antonius Melissa, *Commonplaces* 2.71 = fr. 470. There is a similar anecdote in Diogenes Laertius' account of the life of Diogenes the Cynic at 6.54.

140 Stobaeus, *Anthology* 3.31.10 = fr. 469.

141 See Millett 2007: 74.

142 On the use of the term 'freeborn', which carries a 'strong emotional charge' and is used to arouse indignation see Dover 1974: 286.

143 Diggle 2004: 319.

144 Further analysis in Millett 2007: 58–9.

145 On shameful behaviour caused by inappropriate interaction with slaves see Millett 2007: 73–6, also inappropriate behaviour as the head of the household (77–8), childish behaviour (78–9), inappropriate relationship with a *hetaira* (79) and inappropriate behaviour at the law courts (90–2).

146 Shame can also be misplaced. Theophrastus' *Oligarchic Man* feels ashamed when he is sitting next to a scrawny fellow in the Assembly who has not oiled himself: 26.4–5. This feeling of shame is unwarranted and prompted by the *Oligarchic Man*'s own feelings of superiority. On shame generally see also Halliwell 2004 and Martin in Bilde: esp. 119.

147 Fortenbaugh 2011: 311.

148 On Theophrastus' generosity to his friends see the terms of his will in DL 5.55–56 = fr 1. On his work ethic and reputation for studiousness see DL 5.40 = fr 1 and his list of works at DL 5.42–51. On his conduct see Aulus Gellius, *Attic Nights* 13.5.9–11 = fr. 8. On his appearance see Athenaeus, *The Sophists at Dinner* 1.38 21A – B = fr. 12.

149 Smeed 1985: 275–6.

References

Baltussen, H. 2016. *The Peripatetics: Aristotle's Heirs 322 BCE–200 CE* (London: Routledge).

Boyce, B. 1967. *The Theophrastan Character in England to 1642* (London: Frank Cass & Co).

Bryant, J. M. 1996. *Moral Codes and Social Structure in Ancient Greece* (Albany: State University of New York Press).

Crisp, R. and T. J. Saunders. 1999. 'Aristotle: Ethics and Politics'. In D. Furley (ed.) *From Aristotle to Augustine: Routledge History of Philosophy Vol II* (London: Routledge): 109–146.

Diggle, J. 2004. *Theophrastus: Characters* (Cambridge: Cambridge University Press).

Dover, K. J. 1974. *Greek Popular Morality in the Time of Plato and Aristotle* (Oxford: Basil Blackwell).

Ferguson, J. 1958. *Moral Values in the Ancient World* (London: Methuen).

Fortenbaugh, W. W. 1969. 'Aristotle: Emotion and Moral Virtue', *Arethusa* 2.2: 163–185.

Fortenbaugh, W. W. 1971. 'Aristotle: Animals, Emotion and Moral Virtue', *Arethusa* 4.2: 137–165.

Fortenbaugh, W. W. 1975. 'Aristotle's Analysis of Friendship: Function and Analogy, Resemblance, and Focal Meaning', *Phronesis* 20.1: 51–62.

Fortenbaugh, W. W. 1990. 'Theophrastus, fr. 534 FHS&G' in *Synthesis Philosophica* 10: 457–468 (reprinted in TS: 150–161).

Fortenbaugh, W. W. 1993. 'Theophrastus on Law, Virtue and the Particular Situation'. In R.M. Rosen and J. Farrell (eds) *Nomodeiktes: Greek Studies in Honor of Martin Ostwald* (Ann Arbor: The University of Michigan Press): 447–455.

Fortenbaugh, W. W. 2003a. 'Theophrastus on Emotion' in TS: 71–90.

Fortenbaugh, W. W. 2003b. 'The *Characters* of Theophrastus, Behavioral Regularities and Aristotelian Vices' in TS: 131–145.

Fortenbaugh, W. W. 2011. *Theophrastus of Eresus*. Commentary Volume 6.1. Sources on Ethics (Leiden: Brill).

Furley, D. J. 1953. 'The Purpose of Theophrastus' *Characters*', *SO* 30.1: 56–60.

Glucker, J. 1998. 'Theophrastus, the Academy and the Athenian Philosophical Atmosphere'. In *RUSCH* Vol. VIII: 299–316.

Halliwell, S. 2004. 'Aischrology, Shame, and Comedy'. In I. Sluiter and R.M. Rosen (eds) *Free Speech in Classical Antiquity* (Leiden, Boston: Brill): 115–144.

Halliwell, S. 2008. *Greek Laughter: A Study of Cultural Psychology from Homer to Early Christianity* (Cambridge: Cambridge University Press).

Hughes, G. J. 2001. *Routledge Philosophy Guidebook to Aristotle on Ethics* (London: Routledge).

Ierodiakonou, K. 2016. 'Theophrastus'. *Stanford Encyclopedia of Philosophy*, at https://plato.stanford.edu/entries/theophrastus/ [Accessed January 2017].

Konstan, D. 1997. *Friendship in the Classical World* (Cambridge: Cambridge University Press).

Konstan, D. 2010. 'Are Fellow Citizens Friends? Aristotle versus Cicero on *Philia, Amicitia*, and Social Solidarity'. In R.M. Rosen and I. Sluiter (eds) *Valuing Others in Classical Antiquity* (Leiden, Boston: Brill): 233–248.

Lane Fox, R. J. 1996. 'Theophrastus' Characters and the Historian', *PCPhS* 142: 127–170.

MacIntyre, A. 1998. *A Short History of Ethics: A History of Moral Philosophy from the Homeric Age to the 20th Century* (2nd ed.) (London: Routledge).

Martin, D.B. 1997. 'Hellenistic Superstition'. In P. Bilde et al. (eds) *Conventional Values of the Hellenistic Greeks* (Aarhus: Aarhus University Press): 110–127.

Miller, J. (ed.) 2011. *Aristotle's Nicomachean Ethics: A Critical Guide* (Cambridge: Cambridge University Press).

Millett, P. 1989. 'Patronage and Its Avoidance in Classical Athens'. In A. Wallace-Hadrill (ed.) *Patronage in Ancient Society* (London: Routledge): 15–47.

Millett, P. 1991. *Lending and Borrowing in Ancient Athens* (Cambridge: Cambridge University Press).

Millett, P. 2007. *Theophrastus and His World*. Proceedings of the Cambridge Philological Society Supplementary Volume 33 (Cambridge: Cambridge University Press).

Navarre, O. 1924. *Caractères de Théophraste: commentaire exégétique et critique* (Paris: Les Belles Lettres).

Petersen, E. 1859. *Theophrasti Characteres* (Leipzig: Teubner).

Regenbogen, O. 1940. 'Theophrastos', RE Suppl. 7: 1354–1562.

Rusten, J. and I. C. Cunningham. 2002. *Theophrastus Characters, Herodas Mimes, Sophron and Other Mime Fragments* (Cambridge, MA: Harvard University Press).

Smeed, J. W. 1985. *The Theophrastan 'Character': The History of a Literary Genre* (Oxford: Clarendon Press).

Sollenberger, M. G. 1992. 'The Lives of the Peripatetics: An Analysis of the Contents and Structure of Diogenes Laertius' Vitae philosophorum Book 5', *ANRW* II 36.6: 3793–3879.

Steinmetz, P. 1959. 'Der Zweck der Charaktere Theophrasts', *Annales Universitatis Saraviensis. Philosophie* VIII: 209–246.

Ussher, R. G. 1960. *The Characters of Theophrastus* (London: Macmillan & Co).

Volt, Ivo. 2010. 'Not Valuing Others; Reflections of Social Cohesion in the Characters of Theophrastus'. In R. M. Rosen and I. Sluiter (eds) *Valuing Others in Classical Antiquity* (Leiden: Brill): 303–322.

Williams, B. 1993. *Shame and Necessity* (Berkeley: University of California Press).

5   Style, delivery and the role of character in rhetoric

This chapter deals with three related topics: the style of Theophrastus' writing in the *Characters*, how Theophrastus may have delivered and presented his character types in front of an audience, and the role of character portraits in rhetorical speeches more generally. Theophrastus' style of writing in the *Characters* has attracted widespread criticism but it has several merits, especially simplicity, clarity, brevity and compactness. In the words of one learned commentator, "[t]he art is of a kind that conceals art." [1] In this chapter, we explore the idea that Theophrastus may have presented his character portraits to audiences both within and outside of the Peripatos, and we consider how the character portraits lend themselves to performance and mimicry. Lastly, we will consider how character portraits could be incorporated into rhetorical arguments, such as Theophrastus' amusing character portrait of the 'typical wife' from his treatise on marriage.

A matter of style

Theophrastus' character portraits follow a type of formulaic template. The title of the character type is followed by the statement 'the X man is the sort of person who . . . ' and a series of short clauses describing the characteristic actions of the type in various settings. These clauses are introduced by conjunctions (usually 'and' and sometimes 'next') and occasionally punctuated by phrases such as 'he is apt to' or 'of course he does X' until the description ends, either abruptly or with a comic punchline. The only variation on this formula is the description of the *Coward*, which is presented as a coherent narrative in two different settings (at sea and on the battlefield) and character portraits that consist mainly of quoted or reported speech (such as the *Slanderer* and the *Chatterbox*).[2]

The style of Theophrastus' writing in the *Characters*, although distinctive, has not been well regarded by many modern translators and commentators. According to Ussher, "the Greek is not Greek at its most limpid."[3] Vellacott claims that "[t]he Greek is sometimes obscure or inelegant, the vocabulary colloquial, the style unvaried and abrupt."[4] Boyce states that the presentation of "data" is lacking in subtlety,[5] Jebb says that the style is "incompatible with work of the highest kind"[6] and Trenkner describes part of the work as "a monotonous series . . . of infinitive phrases".[7]

These negative judgements of Theophrastus' writing style in the *Characters* are at odds with Theophrastus' reputation (in the ancient world) for eloquence. Aristotle is said to have renamed Theophrastus to reflect his 'divine' manner of speaking.[8] Diogenes Laertius describes Theophrastus as a "lover of words"[9] and reports that one of Theophrastus' apophthegms was that "one ought sooner trust in an unbridled horse than in disorganized speech".[10] One anecdote suggests that Theophrastus was easily identifiable as a non-Athenian not because he spoke Attic Greek poorly but because he spoke it *too* well.[11] Furthermore, in Theophrastus' work *On Style*,[12] he is said to have discussed four virtues of style, including correct Greek, clarity, appropriateness and ornament.[13] He also distinguished between three stylistic modes[14] as well as words that are pleasant versus those that are "paltry and mean".[15] Taken together, the ancient sources suggest that Theophrastus was well aware of the importance of style and expression.

Furthermore, we know that Theophrastus wrote extensively on the subject of rhetoric[16] and both Cicero[17] and Quintilian[18] compare him to Aristotle, at least in terms of the extent of his output on the subject of rhetoric. Theophrastus wrote three general works on rhetoric (*On the Art of Rhetoric*,[19] *On Kinds of Rhetorical Arts*[20] and *Rhetorical Precepts*[21]) as well as works on invention.[22] He wrote treatises dealing with law court oratory as well as display oratory (*On Praise, On Slander*). He also produced treatises on technical topics and subjects of particular interest to him including his works *On Style, On Delivery* and *On Clamor*.[23]

How then can the apparent contradiction between Theophrastus' reputation for eloquence and his style of writing in the *Characters* be resolved? Certainly, the style of Theophrastus' *Characters* did not prevent the work from being widely admired by later generations of character writers who worked hard to imitate, if not better, his style.[24] It seems we must consider the possibility that Theophrastus' style has been misunderstood or, at least, unduly criticised. I suggest that Theophrastus' style is the result of a careful and deliberate choice. Moreover, it can be defended on the grounds of clarity, simplicity and brevity,[25] and it shows a skilful use of 'cataloguing' and rhetorical technique.

Theophrastus achieves clarity by means of simple expression. He does not attempt (to use one of Theophrastus' own expressions), attempt not to "beautify a pestle".[26] The style befits the subject matter, mirroring the unrefined manners and lack of social intelligence demonstrated by many of his character types. In his portrait of the *Offensive Man*, for example, Theophrastus' uncomplicated style suits the coarseness of the character type:

> He wipes his nose while eating, scratches himself while sacrificing, discharges <spit> from his mouth while talking, belches at you while drinking, does not wash before going to bed with his wife, and uses rancid oil at the baths so that he reeks of the pig-sty.

> (19.5–6)

A grander or weightier style would be entirely inappropriate to the character type. It would also be less conducive to humour and would distract the audience from the conduct being described. Sources indicate that Theophrastus criticised esteemed Athenian orators, such as Isocrates, for failing to adopt an appropriately simple style to suit their subject matter.[27] Theophrastus also criticised the Athenian speech-writer Lysias for using poetic and charming words that were ill-suited to the serious purpose of his speech. Theophrastus reportedly said: "it seems unbecoming when a man seriously engaged in real issues plays with words and by his style does away with emotional effect, for he loses his listener."[28]

Apart from clarity and straightforwardness, Theophrastus relies on everyday forms of speech and expression to illustrate behavioural traits and to make his character types appear more realistic. The *Ungrateful Grumbler* frequently uses 'but' and 'if' to point out the negative aspects of a situation (17.3, 5, 6, 7) while the *Talker* constantly interjects with phrases such as 'Don't forget what you are leading up to', 'Thanks for reminding me' and 'You're quick to grasp the point' (7.3). If Theophrastus does adopt a grander or weightier style, it is often to ridicule the pompous manner of speech adopted by certain types. The *Oligarchic Man* speaks in a manner that suits his political prejudices, uttering dramatic statements like, 'We must meet and discuss this on our own and be rid of the mob' and, 'It's either them or us: we can't both live in this city' (26.3). When the *Man of Petty Ambition* speaks, he uses the type of solemn and formal language one would expect of a politician making a major announcement in the Assembly ('Men of Athens, my colleagues and I') but he has nothing of any consequence to report (21.11).[29]

Theophrastus' character portraits are also excellent illustrations of brevity and compactness. Theophrastus explicitly advocated an economical use of language[30] and he apparently said that words should be carefully and precisely chosen because "well-knit words" are more persuasive.[31] In the *Characters*, Theophrastus can develop a complex character portrait, with details of a man's diet, dress, voice, habits and mannerisms, in just twenty-six words.[32] Although Theophrastus' descriptions of typical behavioural traits can be exceedingly brief, they are still vivid and precise. Consider the following examples: '[w]hen he stubs his toe in the street he is apt to curse the offending stone' (*The Self-Centred Man*, 15.8), 'as a guest at a wedding he delivers a tirade against the female sex' (*The Tactless Man*, 12.6), and, 'he is apt to raid the larder and drink his wine neat' (*The Country Bumpkin*, 4.6). This precise and compact style is evident not only in Theophrastus' *Characters* but in several of his other extant works.[33]

According to Theophrastus, the advantage of a compact style is that rather than setting out every detail for the reader, it allows the reader to become an active and creative participant in the process, filling in gaps for her/himself. In his treatise *On Style*, Theophrastus described this technique as essential for the orator:

[Theophrastus says that] one ought not to elaborate everything in detail, but leave some things for the listener, too, to perceive and infer for himself; for when he perceives what you have left out, he not only is a listener but also becomes your witness, and in addition more favourably disposed. For he thinks himself perceptive, because you have provided him with the occasion to exercise perception. Saying everything as if to a fool gives the appearance of despising the listener.[34]

Theophrastus was clearly aware of the importance of audience psychology and audience involvement.[35] In the *Characters*, Theophrastus' minimalist descriptions provide a bare outline of each type allowing the listener to infer or imagine further details, such as the likely reactions of others to the behaviour. This improves listener participation and enjoyment and encourages the listener to feel more favourably disposed towards the speaker.

Another striking feature of Theophrastus' style is the 'catalogue' technique;[36] that is, a series of short clauses introduced by the conjunction 'and'.[37] In the sketch of the *Illiberal Man*, for example, Theophrastus uses this technique to present a type who is obsessed with avoiding expense and preserving his property:

[And] he stays in the house when he sends out his cloak to the laundry. . . . [And] he wears shoes whose soles have been stitched back on and claims that they are as strong as horn. [And] when he gets up in the morning he sweeps the house and debugs the couches. [And] when he sits down he turns up his tunic, which is all that he is wearing.

(22.8–13)

The recurrence of 'and' in successive clauses is obvious in the original Greek text but it is often edited out of translations of the *Characters*. However, this repetition is an important part of Theophrastus' technique because it emphasises the recurring and tiresome behavioural manifestations of the character types.

Theophrastus' extensive use of cataloguing also conveys an impression of unassailable facts.[38] In his scientific works, Theophrastus regularly catalogues examples and this serves to build the factual basis for his observations. Similarly, in the *Characters*, Theophrastus' lists of typical behaviours are presented as a set of factual observations. In line with Theophrastus' broader methodology, the cataloguing technique is a logical way to present his findings about human behavioural traits. Furthermore, the technique helps with comic exaggeration because it creates the impression that the characters engage in these behaviours all the time. In the case of the *Superstitious Man*, for example, it is unlikely that the same man would do *all* these things *all* the time. Yet, the catalogue technique helps to build a credible picture of a consistent type.[39]

Closely related to the cataloguing technique is Theophrastus' fondness for lists of objects. The *Penny-Pincher*, for example, forbids his wife from lending "salt or a lamp-wick or cummin or marjoram or barley meal or fillets or sacrificial grain" (10.13), the *Country Bumpkin* lies awake at night thinking about the "plough, basket, sickle or sack" that he lent to a neighbour (4.11), and the *Superstitious Man* buys "myrtle-wreaths, frankincense and cakes" (16.10). These lists of objects emphasise the excess or deficiency of the character trait being described because the objects themselves are either of trifling importance or inappropriately excessive.

Although Theophrastus has been criticised for an excessive use of lists, cata-logues and repetitive phrasing, these techniques have a firm foundation in rhetori-cal practice. The technique of repeating the same word or phrase at the beginning of successive clauses, for example, was commonly used to build up to a main punchline or argument.[40] This rhetorical figure of speech works well in the *Char-acters* to create a continuous, flowing narrative and to build comic impact, as examples are layered one upon another and the behaviour appears more and more ridiculous as the description proceeds.

In short, the style of the *Characters* is the result of careful consideration and it is more effective than has hitherto been recognised. As a new type of work, combin-ing comedy and ethics, Theophrastus' *Characters* warranted a new and distinctive style.[41] Accordingly, Theophrastus' style of writing in the *Characters* is quite unique in Greek literature. At the same time, the work reflects key aspects of style – namely, clarity, simplicity, everyday speech and brevity – as well as a fifth aspect in which Theophrastus proved to be truly masterful: compactness. In those instances where the text is inelegant and clumsy, it is no doubt due to the many re-workings, additions and interpolations made by later authors and in these instances, as Diggle has sug-gested, we have every right to be "dissatisfied and suspicious".[42] Editors have done the best they can with the exceedingly corrupt manuscripts[43] and, despite lingering deficiencies with the text, the merits of Theophrastus' style still shine through.

Delivery

Demosthenes, one of the foremost Athenian orators of the fourth century and a con-temporary of Theophrastus, is reported to have been asked for his opinion on the first-, second- and third-most important quality of a good orator. His reply was emphatically repetitive: "Delivery, delivery, delivery".[44] By delivery, Demosthenes was referring to the proper modulation of the voice, proper posture, gestures and facial expressions.[45] But delivery was not a subject of detailed study for rhetoricians before Aristotle, and even though Aristotle admitted its importance,[46] his treatment of the subject was mini-mal. In fact, Aristotle appears to have held a rather dim view of the role of delivery.[47] Aristotle compares the effect of delivery to that of acting and suggests that were it not for the baseness of the audience (and their susceptibility to being persuaded by "mere display"), the subjects of style and delivery would not be very relevant.[48]

According to Fortenbaugh, Theophrastus took a different view and he was, in effect, the first to embrace the subject of delivery and to give it 'technical status'.[49] Theophrastus wrote a work on the subject of delivery,[50] and although we do not know the extent of this work, there are important fragments in later sources that provide some insights into Theophrastus' views. In particular, these fragments suggest that Theophrastus' work on delivery may have been applicable not only to orators but also to actors, musicians and other performers.[51] One fragment indi-cates that, for Theophrastus, effective delivery involved both voice and bodily movement,[52] which brings oratory close to the art of acting:

> Theophrastus the philosopher says . . . that delivery is for an orator the great-est (help) in regard to persuasion. (He says this) referring to the principles and

the emotions of the soul and the knowledge of these, so that the movement of the body and the pitch of the voice are in harmony with the entire science.[53]

This passage demonstrates that, unlike Aristotle, Theophrastus recognised the importance of good delivery in persuading an audience. Theophrastus also understood that an orator needs to have a sound knowledge of emotions and human psychology and that effective delivery involves consideration of a whole range of factors, from tone and facial expression to voice and gesture.[54] According to Plutarch, Theophrastus described hearing as the most emotional of all the senses[55] and said that the voice can be altered from its usual inflection by different emotional states.[56]

In a separate fragment from Cicero's work *On the Orator*, Cicero reports the following:

> For delivery is entirely concerned with the soul, and facial expression is an image of the soul, (and) the eyes informants. For this is the one part of the body which can produce as many signs and changes as there are (e)motions of the soul. In fact there isn't anyone who can produce the same effects with his eyes closed. Theophrastus indeed says that a certain Tauriscus used to say that one who in delivery makes his speech while gazing fixedly upon something is "an actor with his back turned".[57]

Interestingly, this passage directly compares the importance of facial expression and eye contact in rhetorical performance with acting on stage. In this passage, Theophrastus appears to be citing the views of Tauriscus with approval and, if this is the case, it suggests that Theophrastus was more comfortable than Aristotle in recognising a close relationship between oratory and acting. In fact, the treatise that Theophrastus wrote on the subject of delivery may have dealt with both of these applications.[58]

In the lecture room at the Peripatos, Theophrastus was notorious for his lively mode of delivering lectures:

> Hermippus says that Theophrastus used to arrive punctually at the Peripatos, looking splendid and all decked out. Then sitting down, he (used to) present his lecture, refraining from no movement nor any gesture. And once while imitating a gourmet, having stuck out his tongue, he repeatedly licked his lips.[59]

Theophrastus' imitation of the gourmet illustrates his willingness to 'perform' as different character types,[60] a willingness that directly contravenes Aristotle's views about the inappropriateness of gesture for a cultivated audience. Yet, Theophrastus' innovative approach may have been welcomed by his students, contributing to Theophrastus' popularity and his reputedly large student numbers.[61] Outside of the Peripatos, this type of lively delivery would have been appealing to a broader audience as well – the same audience, in fact, who enjoyed watching performances in the theatre.

Given this background, it is easy to imagine Theophrastus incorporating lively gestures and movements into his presentation of the various character types.[62] The *Characters* contain many vivid and humorous examples of behaviour which would be suitable for 'acting out' in the course of lectures: for example, the *Toady* picking lint off his companion's clothes (2.3) or stuffing his own cloak into his mouth to contain his laughter at a feeble joke (2.4). There is also the *Country Bumpkin* who stands dumbstruck in the middle of the road at the sight of an ox, donkey or goat (4.5); the *Superstitious Man* who shudders and spits down at his chest (16.15); and the *Offensive Man* who wipes his nose while eating and scratches himself while sacrificing (19.5).

In those instances where the character descriptions do not lend themselves to the imitation of actions and gestures, there is usually a great deal of quoted speech and therefore plenty of opportunity for mimicry. Theophrastus may have alternated between his own voice (as the narrator), and his character's voices (which vary greatly in pitch, tone and volume) and this would have added greatly to the comic effect.[63] The *Country Bumpkin* is described as speaking 'at the top of his voice' (4.2), the *Toady* 'leans forward and whispers in [his host's] ear' (2.10) while the *Friend of Villains* speaks 'sarcastically' (29.4). There is also the *Shabby Profiteer*, who speaks harshly to his slave (30.8); the *Disagreeable Man*, who uses baby-talk in addressing his child (20.5); the *Self-Centred Man*, who barks at people when asked how he is (15.3); and the *Obsequious Man*, who addresses his friend as "My dear sir" (5.2).

In fact, many concerns about the style of the work are automatically resolved if we allow ourselves to imagine the *Characters* being recited and performed by Theophrastus before an audience, either in the Peripatos or outside of it. The repetition of conjunctions and the succession of short clauses, which can seem monotonous on the printed page, come to life when spoken and performed aloud, particularly if the descriptions are accompanied by gestures and if the speech involves mimicry. Aristotle noted this difference between the spoken and written word in his own work on *Rhetoric*.[64] What Aristotle noted in theory, Theophrastus very likely demonstrated in practice in presenting his *Characters* to an audience.

Characterisation

In the fourth century CE, the rhetoricians Hermogenes and Aphthonius incorporated Theophrastus' *Characters* into their rhetorical handbooks,[65] presumably because they believed that the work could be useful to orators learning how to delineate character.[66] Thanks to this view, the text of the *Characters* was preserved.[67] But does this fact necessarily indicate that the *Characters* was written as a handbook of character types for students of rhetoric?[68] A number of scholars have argued in favour of this view.[69] In my view, Theophrastus did not write the *Characters* primarily for the purposes of rhetoric but this is not to say that the *Characters* could not be *useful* for students of rhetoric.[70] I maintain that they could be useful to budding orators in two ways: firstly, in demonstrating how to identify examples of behaviour that indicate a negative character trait, and secondly, in providing a set of character portraits that could be incorporated into rhetorical arguments.

Plato, who was probably Theophrastus' first teacher, regarded the study of different characters as critically important for successful rhetoric. In Plato's *Phaedrus*, Socrates explains that the genuine art of rhetoric depends upon a true understanding of the innermost nature of men.[71] The student of rhetoric therefore needs to be acquainted with various types of men.[72] A theoretical knowledge of types of character comes first, followed by the categorisation, observation and definition of types in actual life.[73] Later sources indicate that Theophrastus followed this view and recognised the importance of an orator achieving what he calls "rightness in characterization".[74] In his *Rhetoric*, Aristotle subdivided the topic of character according to the effect of emotions on character;[75] the impact of age on character;[76] and the effects of wealth, power and status at birth.[77] By identifying and categorising types of men in his *Characters*, not in theoretical or abstract terms, but as a study of realistic types in everyday life, Theophrastus added to Aristotle's analysis and laid the foundations for one of the central tasks of rhetorical training according to Plato.[78]

Having categorised and defined various types of men, an orator could put this knowledge of character types to good use whenever he needed to cast an opponent as a particular type of individual.[79] To this end, Theophrastus' character portraits offered a series of useful examples of the sorts of behaviours that accompany negative behavioural types.[80] If an orator wanted to cast his opponent as arrogant, for example, Theophrastus' portrait of the *Arrogant Man* demonstrates how to illustrate that trait by focussing on the man's disdainful treatment of others, both in public and private. Similarly, if an orator wanted to cast a legal or political opponent as villainous, Theophrastus' portrait of the *Friend of Villains* demonstrates how to focus on a man's choice of friends and his inclination to defend them. Similarly, Theophrastus' portrait of the *Oligarchic Man* could be adapted if an orator wished to represent a political opponent as having oligarchic sympathies.

By presenting an opponent as a 'type', a skilled orator could cultivate a negative attitude towards an opponent, relying on relatively superficial evidence drawn from a person's behaviour, appearance and manners of speech. In the law courts and in the public assembly, this could be crucial in order to persuade a jury or group of citizens to adopt a negative view of an opponent.[81] This sort of characterisation, even though it may have been exaggerated or inaccurate, was common in ancient rhetoric and it could be highly effective and persuasive.[82]

Theophrastus' negative character portraits could also have been useful for the purposes of rhetorical slander.[83] Slander was a legitimate and formal genre of rhetoric with methods akin to those used in comic caricature and acting,[84] and Theophrastus wrote a work on the subject.[85] Speeches of slander concentrated on particular vices or deficiencies (such as cowardice and intemperance), physical defects (such as weakness and ugliness) and external circumstances (such as poverty or bad friends). Theophrastus' character descriptions demonstrate specific examples of vices and deficiencies that could easily be adapted for these purposes.

For example, Theophrastus' *Coward* and *Obtuse Man* demonstrate a lack of courage and practical intelligence, his *Offensive Man* and *Country Bumpkin* demonstrate ugliness and disease, and the *Man of Petty Ambition* and the *Boastful Man* grossly exaggerate their own importance and station in life. The humour of the *Characters* would also fit well with this genre since the combination of slander and humour was not uncommon in law court oratory.[86]

Apart from helping students learn how to present negative traits for the purposes of oratory, Theophrastus' character portraits could also be incorporated into theses or arguments for or against a particular proposition. At the Peripatos, this form of training in the rhetorical arts was fundamentally important.[87] It provided an opportunity for students to develop skills in argumentation and to receive instruction on matters of style, delivery and content.[88] Cicero alludes to the technique of arguing both sides of a proposition as having been established by Aristotle.[89] The technique involved putting forward a thesis or proposal and discovering arguments that would support or destroy the thesis through "probable premises".[90] Both Aristotle and Theophrastus set out these sorts of arguments in their books entitled *Theses*.[91] Theophrastus is recorded by Diogenes Laertius to have written three collections of theses (two simply named *Theses* and one named *Thesis on the Soul*).[92]

Fortunately, a remnant of a thesis written by Theophrastus survives in a later source.[93] It is alleged to have come from Theophrastus' "little golden book *On Marriage*" in which he argues against the proposition that the wise man should marry.[94] The extract artfully demonstrates how a character sketch could be incorporated into a thesis.[95] The character type that forms the foundation for the argument is the 'typical wife', and the similarities between the presentation of this character type and the techniques used in Theophrastus' *Characters* are numerous. Fortenbaugh has identified two similarities (Theophrastus' use of lists and his preference for a clever punchline) but there are many others that may be observed.[96]

Case study: whether the wise man should marry

The thesis begins with a clear statement of the question under consideration, in this case: "should the wise man marry?" It then briefly surveys the circumstances in which a wise man should marry, all of which are contingent upon a confluence of highly favourable (and therefore unrealistic) circumstances: "If the woman is beautiful, if she is well-mannered, if she is of honourable parents, if he himself is healthy and rich, in such circumstances occasionally a wise man should marry." The style of this introductory passage, which repeats the word 'if' and uses short cumulative clauses, reminds one of the style of Theophrastus' *Characters*. This introductory part of the thesis also functions as a kind of rhetorical concession by means of "which the speaker seeks to establish himself as a reasonable person".[97] But it is also typical of Theophrastus to set out an ideal and then to contrast it with the reality (as we saw with Theophrastus' views on friendship in Chapter 4). Theophrastus concludes that because the ideal is rarely attainable, "the wise man ought not to marry."

The treatise then proceeds to set out the main arguments against marriage, namely, that wives impede philosophical studies, that they need and expect a great deal, that they complain a lot, that choosing a wife is difficult and that wives are difficult to guard. Each of these arguments is supported by a series of examples and descriptions of the circumstances of married life. The examples are presented in the form of lists and catalogues, which resemble the use of lists and catalogues in Theophrastus' *Characters*, such as when Theophrastus says: "[t]he habits of wives require many things: expensive dresses, gold, jewels, money to spend, maid-servants, various utensils, litters and gilded chariots."[98]

Quoted speech, a favourite technique of Theophrastus' in the *Characters*, is employed to illustrate that the 'typical wife' is suspicious and full of complaints:

> Further, there are garrulous complaints all night long: 'That lady appears in public more elegantly dressed.' 'This lady is respected by everyone. Poor me, I am despised in the company of women.' 'Why were you looking at the woman next door?' 'What were you saying to the young maid?' 'What have you brought me from the marketplace?'

On the difficulties of choosing a wife, Theophrastus again makes good use of rhetorical devices, introducing successive clauses with 'if'. The short phrases accumulate quickly and the unexpected examples add to the comic effect: "If irritable, if foolish, if misshapen, if arrogant, if foul-smelling, whatever her defect, we learn about it after the wedding." Theophrastus also uses repetition in successive clauses to create rhythm and a strong emotional effect:

> Her face *must* always be the subject of attention and her beauty praised. . . . She *must* be called 'Princess'. Her birthday *must* be celebrated. You *must* swear by her health and wish that she outlive you. You *must* honor her nurse and nanny.
>
> (emphasis added)

In the *Characters*, Theophrastus is masterful at comic punchlines, such as the description of the *Talker* that ends with the *Talker*'s children saying: "Talk to us, daddy ... and send us to sleep" (7.10) and the *Chatterbox*, who ends his rambling monologue with the unexpected statement, "I threw up yesterday" (3.3).[99] The same use of unexpected comic punchlines is evident in Theophrastus' thesis on marriage.[100] After listing the household helpers, including a nanny, servant and handsome attendant, Theophrastus unexpectedly adds: "[u]nder these names lurk adulterers". After describing the risks of not allowing one's wife to run the household, Theophrastus says: "unless you take steps quickly, she prepares poison for you." After outlining the problems with guarding a wife, Theophrastus concludes: "it is less irksome to have a misshapen wife than to guard a shapely one."

Theophrastus then presents four possible counter-arguments and addresses each one in turn. In refuting the notion that one should marry for the sake of children, for example, Theophrastus points out that a son provides no certainty since a son may die before his father, or have a perverse character, or be too keen to inherit his father's hard-earned wealth. These concerns are reminiscent of Theophrastus' *Ungrateful Grumbler* who, on hearing of the birth of a son, complains that he is destined to lose half of his property (17.7–8). The treatise ends abruptly with the refutation of the remaining arguments and the case is closed.

The importance of Theophrastus' portrait of the typical wife for our purposes is that it demonstrates how a character portrait could fit neatly into a piece of display oratory. In this case, the character portrait provides the necessary facts to support the main argument and it is drawn quickly, precisely and persuasively. The character portrait involves the use of stylistic devices, such as lists and catalogues, repetition, amplification and quoted speech. These stylistic devices contribute to the persuasiveness of the evidence and its comic presentation. To this end, it hardly matters whether the character sketch is grossly exaggerated, conflates the evidence, or presents isolated instances of behaviour as if they are routine and frequent occurrences. It is all a matter of how artfully the evidence is presented, and an audience that is amused is more likely to be persuaded.

In short, the depiction of the 'typical wife' gives the narrative character. As in Theophrastus' portraits of male types, the portrait of the wife focusses on manner of speech, physical appearance and typical modes of behaviour. The examples of behaviour are linked to everyday activities (such as managing the household and dealing with friends, slaves and visitors), which lends realism and credibility to the observations. There are plentiful instances of comic relief to sustain audience interest and the evidence is presented in a compact but lively style. Furthermore, the character portrait of the 'typical wife', like Theophrastus' descriptions of male types, naturally lends itself towards lively delivery. One can imagine Theophrastus imitating the wife's garrulous and endless complaints, perhaps in a high-pitched voice, or her tortured facial expressions and overly dramatic gestures as she 'advertises' insincere grief over her sick husband.

Theophrastus has moulded the character portrait into a persuasive rhetorical thesis, giving us a clear picture of the character portrait 'in action'. Perhaps Theophrastus' portraits of male character types could be adapted to similar purposes. One can imagine Theophrastus' *Penny-Pincher*, *Illiberal Man* and *Boastful Man* being utilised for a debate about whether the wise man should be concerned with wealth, or the *Dissembler*, *Rumour-Monger* and *Slanderer* providing material for a debate about the importance of truthfulness in speech.

Given that we have largely been concerned with Theophrastus' descriptions of male character types, it seems fair to conclude with a comical portrait of a female character type. In fact, Theophrastus' portrait of the 'typical wife' suggests that he was equally skilled at recognising failings in both men and women.[101] There is no evidence that Theophrastus ever married, so perhaps the arguments that Theophrastus put forward do indeed reflect his personal views, or perhaps the ideal 'Theophrastus Man' proved to be just as elusive as the ideal 'Theophrastus Woman'! Either way, Theophrastus approaches the subject of male and female character types with his unique blend of comic humour and ethical instruction. For Theophrastus personally, as a keen observer of humankind, a practical scientist and a great thinker, it may well be that he found his consolation in the solitary pursuit of philosophy, as his own writings indicate:

> [T]he wise man can never be alone. He has with him everyone who is and who ever was good, and he turns his thoughts freely wherever he wishes. What he cannot physically embrace, he embraces with his mind. And if there is a lack of men, he will speak with God. He will never be less alone than when he is alone.[102]

Notes

1 Smeed 1985: 5.
2 See Boyce 1967: 8.
3 Ussher 1960: 3.
4 Vellacott 1967: 8. According to Millett, Vellacott undercuts his own argument by producing an "eminently readable translation": Millett 2007: 16.
5 Boyce 1967: 9.
6 Jebb-Sandys: 23.
7 Trenkner 1958: 148.
8 See DL 5.38 = fr. 1 at line 30, also see frs. 5–7.
9 The term used is '*philologos*': see DL 5.37 = fr. 1 at line 13.
10 DL 5.39–40 = fr. 1 at lines 41–2.
11 Cicero, *Brutus* 172 = fr. 7A and Quintilian, *Oratorical Education* 8.1.2 = fr. 7B. See discussion in Millett 2007: 1–2.
12 DL 5.47 = fr. 1 = 666 no. 17a.
13 Cicero, *Orator* 79 = fr. 684. Correct Greek was Theophrastus' innovation. The remaining three virtues had already been discussed by Aristotle: see Fortenbaugh 2005: 422. Also Johnstone 1996: 126.
14 Dionysius of Halicarnassus, *On Demosthenes* 3 = fr. 685. Discussion in Hendrickson 1904, Kennedy 1957, Kennedy 1994: 86 and Walker 2000: 47. Consistent with his ethical approach, Theophrastus advocated the mean or 'middle' style: see Innes 1985: 262.
15 Demetrius, *On Style* 173–5 = fr. 687 and Dionysius of Halicarnassus, *On Literary Composition* 16 = fr. 688.
16 See the list of titles at fr. 666.1–24.
17 See Cicero, *On the Orator* 1.43 = fr. 667.
18 Quintilian, *Oratorical Education* 3.1.15 = fr. 670.
19 DL 5.48 = fr. 1 line 234 = 666 no. 1; discussion in Fortenbaugh 2005: 53–7.
20 DL 5.48 = fr. 1 line 235 = 666 no. 2a; discussion in Fortenbaugh 2005: 57–64.
21 DL 5.47 = fr. 1 line 221 = 666 no. 3; see Fortenbaugh 2005: 66–9.
22 See Fortenbaugh 2005: 69ff.
23 See discussion in Fortenbaugh 2005: 49ff. For discussion of the work *On Delivery* see Fortenbaugh 2003b: 268–71 and Fortenbaugh 2003a. Theophrastus' former student and regent of Athens, Demetrius of Phalerum, is reported to have been an excellent orator. See Quintilian, *Inst. Orat.* 10.1.80 and Cicero *De Orat* 2.95 as discussed in Sollenberger 2000: 313. He is also said to have shared Theophrastus' interests in the subject of diction and delivery: see O'Sullivan 2009: 232.
24 Ussher 1960: 31.
25 On these virtues of style see Dionysius of Halicarnassus, *On Lysias* 6 = fr. 695.
26 See Demetrius, *On Style* 114 = fr. 686; also Grube 1961: 114, 119.
27 Dionysius of Halicarnassus, *On Isocrates* 3 = fr. 691.
28 Dionysius of Halicarnassus, *On Lysias* 14 = fr. 692.

29 For a detailed analysis of this scene see Diggle 2004: 23–5.
30 Dionysius of Halicarnassus, *On Lysias* 6 = fr. 695; see discussion by Fortenbaugh 2005: 423, 309.
31 Cicero, *Orator* 228 = fr. 699.
32 See the *Country Bumpkin*, as discussed by Diggle 2004: 20–1.
33 See for example his treatises *On the Senses*, *On Stones* and *On Fire*. Admittedly, there may be particular reasons for a compact style in scientific treatises (especially if the subject does not warrant lengthy treatment or if the work is an unfinished series of fieldnotes) but compactness seems to be a fairly consistent feature of Peripatetic writings.
34 Demetrius, *On Style* 222 = fr. 696.
35 Fortenbaugh 2005: 423.
36 See Smeed 1985: 279–80.
37 Anderson describes the repeated use of 'and' as extremely bad style by the standards of earlier Greek prose: Anderson 1970: vii. However, it is not so troublesome when viewed in the context of rhetorical performance and it was described with approval as a rhetorical method by Demetrius (student of Theophrastus): see Grube 1961: 59.
38 On 'cataloguing' as a stylistic device see Hoggart 1970: 46.
39 See Millett 2007: 39.
40 Fortenbaugh 2003a: 228.
41 Lane Fox 1996: 139.
42 Diggle 2004: 25.
43 Diggle 2004: 20.
44 Cicero, *Brutus*, 38, 142; *Orator* 56; *De Oratore* 3.213.
45 Corbett and Connors 1999: 17–23.
46 *Rh.* 3.3 (1403b).
47 See Fortenbaugh 2007. Also see Worman 2008: 278, 287–90.
48 *Rh.* 3.2–5 (1403b–1404a). See also Aristotle's *Poetics*, 1461b–1462a.
49 Fortenbaugh 2005: 426. Also see Fortenbaugh 2003b: 254.
50 DL 5.48 = fr. 1, line 236 = 666 no. 24.
51 Fortenbaugh 2003b: 271.
52 Fortenbaugh 2003b: 257.
53 Athanasius, *Prefatory Remarks to Hermogenes' On Issues* = fr. 712. Discussed in Fortenbaugh 2005: 397ff.
54 See Worman 2008: 278.
55 Plutarch, *On the Right Way to Listen to Lectures* 2 37F–38A = fr. 293; Fortenbaugh 2003b: 258.
56 Plutarch, *Table Talk* 1.5.2 623A = fr. 719A; see Fortenbaugh 2003b: 258.
57 Cicero, *On the Orator* 3.221 = fr. 713; see Fortenbaugh 2005: 413–15.
58 On some difficulties interpreting this passage see Fortenbaugh 2003b: 260.
59 Athenaeus, *The Sophists at Dinner* 1.38 21A – B = fr. 12.
60 There is also some similarity with ancient Greek mime, which was considered to be an "imitation of base deeds and words": see Diomedes, *The Art of Grammar* 3, Chapter on Poems, 491.13–16 = fr. 708.
61 DL 5.37 = fr. 1 at line 16.
62 See Diggle 2004: 16.
63 On variation in the narrator's and subject's voices see Millett 2007: 116–7.
64 *Rh.* 3.12.2 (1413b).
65 Fortenbaugh 2003a: 227, esp. fn. 14.
66 Fortenbaugh 2003a: 227.
67 See Diggle 2004: 13, n. 42.
68 For a list of supporters of this view see Diggle 2004: 13, n. 41. For similarities with rhetoric, see Immisch 1923: 210–12 and Furley 1953: 59–60.
69 For pertinent criticisms of these views see Lane Fox 1996: 139.
70 See Fortenbaugh 2005: 417.

71 Pl. *Phdr.* 270e.
72 Pl. *Phdr.* 271a.
73 Pl. *Phdr.* 271b.
74 See Quintilian, *Oratorical Education* 10.1.27 = fr. 707.
75 *Rh.* 2.1.8–2.11.7 (1378a–1388b).
76 *Rh.* 2.12.1–2. 14.4 (1389a–1390b).
77 *Rh.* 2.15.1–2.17.6 (1390b–1391b).
78 Fortenbaugh sees even closer parallels between Plato's *Phaedrus* and Theophrastus' *Characters*: see Fortenbaugh 2003a: 228–31.
79 See Fortenbaugh 2003a: 228.
80 See Fortenbaugh 2005: 421.
81 See Trenkner 1958: 148.
82 See Arena 2007.
83 Aristotle dismisses the speech of slander as 'obvious', since it is based on the opposite points to the speech of praise: see *Rh.* 1.9.41 (1368a). See also Worman 2008: 277ff.
84 Worthington 1994: 198.
85 DL 5.46 = fr. 1, line 189 = 666 n. 13.
86 Worthington 1994: 201.
87 Fortenbaugh 2003a: 231.
88 Fortenbaugh 2003a: 232.
89 Cicero, *On Ends* 5.10 = fr. 672.
90 Alexander of Aphrodisias, *On Aristotle's* Topics 1.2 101a26 = fr. 135.
91 Aelius Theon, *Preliminary Exercises* 2 = fr. 74.
92 Crantor is alleged to have jibed that Theophrastus wrote his theses in purple ink: see Diogenes Laertius, *The Lives of the Philosophers* 4.27 = fr. 75, while Lynceus is alleged to have described Theophrastus' theses as 'sheer happiness': see Hippolochus, *Letter to Lynceus*, in Athenaeus, *The Sophists at Dinner* 4.5 130D = fr. 76. Satirical tone aside, these comments at least confirm that Theophrastus wrote theses: see Fortenbaugh 2003a: 232.
93 Jerome, *Against Jovinian* 1.47–8 = fr. 486.
94 For a discussion of the possible scope of Theophrastus' book *On Marriage* see Fortenbaugh 2011: 178–181. For a discussion of the fragment's derivation and its appearance in Jerome's work see Schmitt 1971: 260–1.
95 On the extraordinary influence of this excerpt in the Middle Ages and the Renaissance see Schmitt 1971: 262–8.
96 Fortenbaugh 2003a: 233.
97 Fortenbaugh 2003a: 233, fn. 34.
98 Fortenbaugh 2003a: 233.
99 For other examples of direct speech punchlines see character portraits 1.6, 7.10, 8.10, 9.8, 13.11, 14.13, 17.9, 20.10 and 24.13.
100 Fortenbaugh 2003a: 233.
101 Fortenbaugh 2011: 361. Theophrastus' views on women are not all negative. On the value of education for women see Stobaeus, *Anthology* 2.31.31 = fr. 662, and on the possibility of a virtuous wife being a friend to a virtuous husband see Aspasius, *On Aristotle's* Nicomachean Ethics 8.8 1158b11–28 = fr. 533.
102 See Jerome, *Against Jovinian* 1.47–8 = fr. 486, lines 63–66.

References

Anderson, W. 1970. *Theophrastus: The Character Sketches* (Kent, OH: Kent State University Press).

Arena, V. 2007. 'Roman Oratorical Invective'. In W. Dominik and J. Hall (eds). *A Companion to Roman Rhetoric* (Malden, MA: Blackwell): 149–160.

Boyce, B. 1967. *The Theophrastan Character in England to 1642* (London: Frank Cass & Co).

Corbett, E. and R. Connors. 1999. *Classical Rhetoric for the Modern Student* 4th ed. (New York, Oxford: Oxford University Press).

Diggle, J. 2004. *Theophrastus Characters*. Cambridge Classical Texts and Commentaries 43. (Cambridge: Cambridge University Press).

Fortenbaugh, W. W. 2003a. 'Theophrastus, the Characters and Rhetoric' in TS: 224–243.

Fortenbaugh, W. W. 2003b. 'Theophrastus on Delivery' in TS: 253–271.

Fortenbaugh, W.W. 2005. *Theophrastus of Eresus: Sources for his Life, Writings, Thought and Influence*. Commentary Volume 8. Sources on Rhetoric and Poetics, (Leiden: Brill).

Fortenbaugh, W.W. 2007. 'Aristotle's Art of Rhetoric'. In I. Worthington (ed.) *A Companion to Greek Rhetoric* (Malden, MA; Oxford: Blackwell): 107–123.

Fortenbaugh, W.W. 2011. Theophrastus of Eresus. Commentary Volume 6.1. *Sources on Ethics* (Leiden: E.J. Brill).

Furley, D. J. 1953. 'The Purpose of Theophrastus' *Characters*', *SO* 30.1: 56–60.

Grube, G. 1961. *A Greek Critic: Demetrius on Style* (Toronto: University of Toronto Press).

Hendrickson, G. L. 1904. 'The Peripatetic Mean of Style', *AJPh* 25: 125–146.

Hoggart, R. 1970. *Speaking to Each Other About Literature Vol. 2* (London: Chatto and Windus).

Immisch, O. 1923. *Theophrasti Characteres* (Leipzig: Teubner).

Innes, D.C. 1985. 'Theophrastus and the Theory of Style'. In *RUSCH* Vol. II: 251–267.

Johnstone, C. L. (ed.) 1996. *Theory, Text, Context: Issues in Greek Rhetoric and Oratory* (New York: State University of New York Press).

Kennedy, G. A. 1957. 'Theophrastus and Stylistic Distinctions', *HSPh* 62: 93–104.

Kennedy, G.A. 1994. *A New History of Classical Rhetoric* (Princeton: Princeton University Press).

Lane Fox, R. 1996. 'Theophrastus' Characters and the Historian', *PCPhS* 42, 127–170.

Millett, P. 2007. *Theophrastus and His World* (Cambridge: Cambridge University Press).

O'Sullivan, L. 2009. *The Regime of Demetrius of Phalerum in Athens, 317–307 BCE: A Philosopher in Politics* (Leiden: E. J. Brill).

Schmitt, C.B. 1971. 'Theophrastus in the Middle Ages', *Viator* 2: 251–270.

Smeed, J. W. 1985. *The Theophrastan 'Character': The History of a Literary Genre* (Oxford: Clarendon Press).

Sollenberger, M.G. 2000. 'Diogenes Laertius' Life of Demetrius of Phalerum'. In *RUSCH* Vol. IX: 311–329.

Trenkner, S. 1958. *The Greek Novella in the Classical Period* (Cambridge: Cambridge University Press).

Ussher, R. G. 1960. *The Characters of Theophrastus* (London: Macmillan & Co).

Vellacott, P. 1967. *Menander: Plays and Fragments, Theophrastus: The Characters* (Harmondsworth, Penguin).

Walker, J. 2000. *Rhetoric and Poetics in Antiquity* (Oxford: Oxford University Press).

Worman, N. 2008. *Abusive Mouths in Classical Athens* (Cambridge: Cambridge University Press).

Worthington, I. 1994. *Persuasion: Greek Rhetoric in Action* (London: Routledge).

6   Epilogue

Conclusions and implications

Theophrastus led a remarkable life as Aristotle's colleague and successor (Chapter 1). He was an astounding polymath, a prolific writer and an innovative thinker. His own unique character as a philosopher, scientist and *metic* shaped his interests, outlook and methodology. While Theophrastus may never be considered equal or superior to Aristotle in his contribution to human knowledge (simply because he came after Aristotle and fewer of his works are extant), he can certainly be viewed as Aristotle's rival in scope and output and as extending Aristotle's theories in important areas.

Among Theophrastus' extant works, the *Characters* stands out as a particularly unique and influential contribution (Chapter 2). Although character portraits had appeared from time to time in Greek literature before the Characters, Theophrastus was certainly the first to write a dedicated book of character portraits and to present them in such a realistic and humorous manner. Theophrastus' method influenced many later authors, including later Peripatetics, Roman satirists and poets, and, in the medieval period, Geoffrey Chaucer. In modern literature, Theophrastus' character portraits have been widely recognised for their value in sensitising the reader to negative characteristics in human behaviour. Writers from La Bruyère to George Eliot have borrowed Theophrastus' technique and analysed characters in their own culture, life and times with the same intention of instruction and entertainment. It is hoped that this book will help to revive interest in the *Characters* in the twenty-first century and promote greater recognition of its remarkable contribution to the field of literature.

While the influence of the *Characters* in literature is readily apparent, the question of Theophrastus' original purpose in writing the *Characters* is more problematic, especially if we try fit the *Characters* into a single defined area of study. To a large extent, this problem is resolved if we allow the *Characters* to relate to multiple fields of study. After all, the Peripatetics studied many subject areas and disciplines simultaneously and these different fields of study were regarded as interrelated and compatible. Theophrastus, for example, applied his method of scientific classification, observation and analysis to the study of natural phenomena as well as to studies of human character, ethics and behaviour. In a similar way, the *Characters* does not belong solely to ethics *or* comedy *or* rhetoric. It represents a unique synthesis of comedy and ethics, with distinct applications for rhetoric as well.

In essence, the purpose of the *Characters* is to convey ethical teaching in a highly practical, amusing and memorable way. As we saw in Chapter 3, Theophrastus had a keen interest in the subject of comedy and he defined the jest as 'a concealed rebuke for error'. The *Characters* can be read as a series of concealed 'rebukes' of negative character traits, artfully softened by the use of comedy, but nonetheless revealing a series of 'errors' that involve a lack of self-awareness. Theophrastus achieves comedy by presenting examples of behaviour in a simple, condensed style that makes good use of comic punchlines, popular speech and occasional vulgarity. Theophrastus' humour is harmless and it has done wonders to ensure the survival of the work over many centuries.

Theophrastus' particular interest in physical and moral deficiencies contributed the 'science' of physiognomy and the theory that a person's character can be deduced from his/her appearance movements and gestures (Chapter 3). In the *Characters*, Theophrastus' interest in physiognomy is reflected in his vivid descriptions of physical attributes but also in his studies of more nuanced cues stemming from gestures, modes of speech and behaviour. These character cues would have been very helpful to students learning how to depict character quickly and artfully for the purposes of dramatic performances. In fact, I have argued that the science of physiognomy had a direct influence upon character portrayal in the comic theatre and the development of more sophisticated masks representing character types. This represents a fascinating area of overlap between Theophrastus' work at the Peripatos and the evolution of the comic theatre in fourth-century Athens.

The best example of Theophrastus' influence on comedy is the surviving work of Menander (Chapter 3). There is little doubt that Menander was Theophrastus' student and that he learned a great deal about character portrayal from Theophrastus. They share a common interest in negative character traits, they adopt similar methods to portray character and they express similar philosophical views, especially on the impact of misfortune on character. Undoubtedly, Menander went on to refine and develop his skills in characterisation as a playwright and he enjoyed great success outside of his early connection with the Peripatos, but it is also likely that Menander's education under Theophrastus contributed to that success.

Theophrastus' comic presentation of the *Characters* is so effective that the work has sometimes been dismissed as nothing more than 'light entertainment'. This view fails to recognise the ethical substructure of the work (Chapter 4). In the character portraits, Theophrastus demonstrates that virtue is not an abstract philosophical concept but one that must be put into practice in daily life and social interaction. Being an eminently practical philosopher, Theophrastus realised that a model of 'bad' behaviour would be just as instructive but more realistic and more memorable than a model of 'good' behaviour. So he devised the *Characters*. Unlike Aristotle's ethical works, Theophrastus offers no analysis or commentary because the 'bad' conduct is self-explanatory and Theophrastus trusts his audience to extract the ethical principle for themselves. Indeed, as we saw in Chapter 4, the

Characters can be read as a guide to certain key social values, especially the value of friendship, love of mankind and feelings of shame.

Underlying Theophrastus' portrayal of inappropriate, ill-timed and poorly judged conduct is also a desire to heighten people's self-awareness (Chapter 3). By shining a spotlight on character types who are unaware of deficiencies that are manifestly obvious to others, Theophrastus hopes to raise people's awareness of these deficiencies and encourage avoidance of them. On an individual level, we laugh openly at the character descriptions but, when the laughter subsides, we may privately reflect on whether we have ever behaved in a similar fashion. At a broader level, shared laughter at the inappropriate behaviour of the character types helps to reinforce social norms and expectations. Laughing at the character types can also have a cathartic effect, replacing negative reactions towards irritating types with a kindlier attitude and a healthier comic outlook (Chapter 3).

Apart from being amusing and instructive, Theophrastus' character portraits were also useful, especially for those learning the skill of characterisation for the purposes of oratory (Chapter 5). Theophrastus shows orators how to observe, define and categorise different character types. He also demonstrates how to portray these types using a simple, compact and effective style. In fact, Theophrastus' style in the *Characters* sits well with his views about the importance of lively delivery and one can imagine Theophrastus acting out his character portraits in a highly entertaining manner for a public audience. In the context of rhetorical debates arguing for or against a particular proposition, the character portrait comes to life. We can see this in Theophrastus' portrait of the 'typical wife', which formed the basis for a rhetorical showpiece arguing against marriage for the wise man.

If one of the hallmarks of great literature is that it is memorable and continues to resonate with us throughout life, then there is little doubt that Theophrastus' *Characters* is such a work. To be sure, the *Characters* provides a unique insight into the people of fourth-century Athens and their social values but it also provides a picture of humanity that can entertain, delight, instruct and resonate with people even in the twenty-first century. After reading the *Characters*, it is virtually impossible to go about one's daily life without referring to the character portraits and to resist becoming a Theophrastean-style observer of the character types peculiar to one's own culture, society and times. Theophrastus' greatest legacy is that he has shown us how to go about this with perceptiveness, humour and a wonderfully philosophical viewpoint.

Index

For Product Safety Concerns and Information please contact our EU representative GPSR@taylorandfrancis.com Taylor & Francis Verlag GmbH, Kaufingerstraße 24, 80331 München, Germany

Printed and bound by CPI Group (UK) Ltd, Croydon, CR0 4YY

08/06/2025

01896991-0014